CALM

THOUGHTS AND QUOTATIONS FOR EVERY DAY

summersdale

CALM

This revised edition copyright © Summersdale Publishers Ltd, 2018

First published in 2010

Summersdale Publishers Ltd
46 West Street
Chichester
West Sussex
PO19 1RP
UK

www.summersdale.com

Printed and bound in the Czech Republic

ISBN: 978-1-78685-242-7

Substantial discounts on bulk quantities of Summersdale books are available to corporations, professional associations and other organisations. For details contact general enquiries: telephone: +44 (0) 1243 771107 or email: enquiries@summersdale.com.

1ST June 2018

To ..... Lynda ....

From .... Fiona ....

Keep your face to
the sunshine and
you cannot see
the shadow.

Helen Keller

There is no joy
but calm!

Alfred, Lord Tennyson

You cannot perceive beauty but with a serene mind.

Henry David Thoreau

Have patience with
ALL THINGS,
but chiefly
have patience
WITH YOURSELF.

St Francis de Sales

There is a serene
and settled majesty
to woodland scenery
that enters into the
soul and delights
and elevates it.

Washington Irving

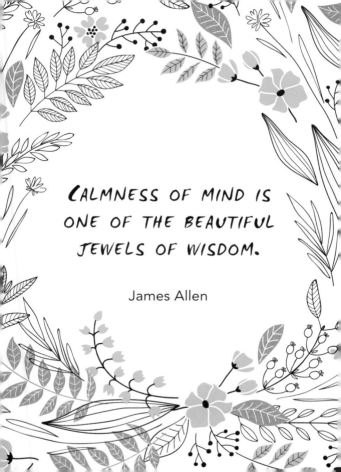

CALMNESS OF MIND IS
ONE OF THE BEAUTIFUL
JEWELS OF WISDOM.

James Allen

Inward calm cannot BE MAINTAINED unless physical strength is constantly and INTELLIGENTLY REPLENISHED.

Buddha

The time to relax is when you don't have time for it.

Sydney J. Harris

A FREE MIND IS ONE
WHICH IS UNTROUBLED AND
UNFETTERED BY ANYTHING.

Meister Eckhart

PEACE IS NOT MERELY A DISTANT GOAL THAT WE SEEK BUT A MEANS BY WHICH WE ARRIVE AT THAT GOAL.

Martin Luther King Jr

Freedom from desire leads to inner peace.

Lao Tzu

WHENEVER YOU ARE SINCERELY PLEASED, YOU ARE NOURISHED.

Ralph Waldo Emerson

That which does
not kill me, makes
me stronger.

Friedrich Nietzsche

TO EVERY PROBLEM
THERE IS ALREADY
A SOLUTION
WHETHER YOU
KNOW IT OR NOT.

Grenville Kleiser

BEAUTIFUL MUSIC IS THE ART OF THE PROPHETS THAT CAN CALM THE AGITATIONS OF THE SOUL.

Martin Luther

For the man sound
in body and serene of
mind there is no such
thing as bad weather;
every sky has
its beauty.

George Gissing

We think in
eternity, but
we move slowly
through time.

Oscar Wilde

A well-spent day
brings happy sleep.

Leonardo da Vinci

LET US
NOT LOOK
BACK IN
ANGER, NOR
FORWARD IN
FEAR, BUT
AROUND IN
AWARENESS.

James Thurber

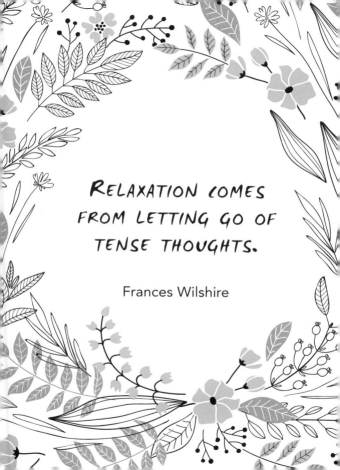

RELAXATION COMES FROM LETTING GO OF TENSE THOUGHTS.

Frances Wilshire

THOSE WHO ARE AT WAR WITH OTHERS ARE NOT AT PEACE WITH THEMSELVES.

William Hazlitt

Be calm in arguing:
for fierceness makes
error a fault, and
truth discourtesy.

George Herbert

Never be in a hurry;
do everything

QUIETLY

and in a

CALM SPIRIT.

St Francis de Sales

Our real blessings
often appear to us
in the shapes of
pains, losses and
disappointments; but
let us have patience,
and we soon shall
see them in their
proper figures.

Joseph Addison

It's better to

LIGHT A CANDLE

than to curse the

DARKNESS.

Anonymous

LET US FOLLOW
OUR DESTINY,
EBB AND FLOW.
WHATEVER
MAY HAPPEN,
WE MASTER
FORTUNE BY
ACCEPTING IT.

Virgil

Nothing can
bring you peace
but yourself.

Ralph Waldo Emerson

No one outside
ourselves can rule
us inwardly. When
we know this, we
become free.

Buddha

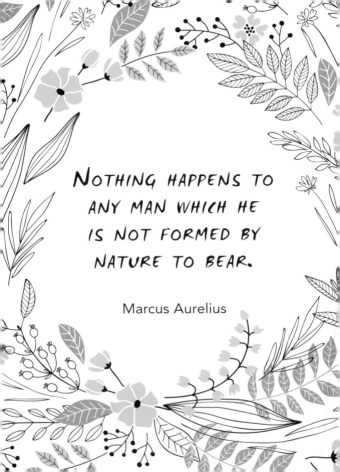

NOTHING HAPPENS TO
ANY MAN WHICH HE
IS NOT FORMED BY
NATURE TO BEAR.

Marcus Aurelius

BE GLAD
OF LIFE
BECAUSE IT
GIVES YOU
THE CHANCE
TO LOVE, TO
WORK, TO
PLAY, AND TO
LOOK UP AT
THE STARS.

Henry van Dyke

A cloudy day is no match for a sunny disposition.

William Arthur Ward

Music alone
with sudden
charms can bind
The wand'ring
sense, and calm
the troubled mind.

William Congreve

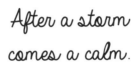

After a storm
comes a calm.

Proverb

Fear cannot be banished, but it can be calm and without panic; it can be mitigated by reason and evaluation.

Vannevar Bush

Calm can solve
all issues.

Pope Shenouda III

TO THE MIND
THAT IS STILL, THE
WHOLE UNIVERSE
SURRENDERS.

Lao Tzu

A heart at peace gives life to the body.

Proverbs 14:30

Perfect tranquillity within consists in the good ordering of the mind, the realm of your own.

Marcus Aurelius

IF YOU ARE IRRITATED
BY EVERY RUB, HOW
WILL YOUR MIRROR
BE POLISHED?

Rumi

CONTROL
WHAT YOU
CAN, BUT
FLOW WITH
WHAT YOU
CAN'T.

Alan Cohen

Better than a
thousand
HOLLOW WORDS,
is one word that
BRINGS PEACE.

Buddha

Things without all
remedy, should be
without regard;
what's done, is done.

William Shakespeare

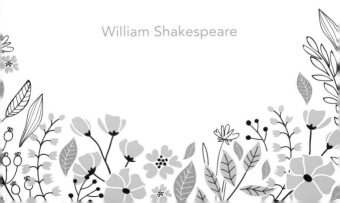

CONTEMPLATION

*is the loving sense
of this life, this*

PRESENCE

and this eternity.

Thomas Merton

Our noisy years seem
moments in the being
Of the eternal
Silence: truths
that wake
To perish never.

William Wordsworth

IT WAS ONLY
FROM AN INNER
CALM THAT MAN
WAS ABLE TO
DISCOVER AND
SHAPE CALM
SURROUNDINGS.

Stephen Gardiner

Nothing in life is
to be feared, it is only
to be understood.

Marie Curie

IN DEEP
MEDITATION
THE FLOW OF
CONCENTRATION
IS CONTINUOUS,
LIKE THE FLOW
OF OIL.

Patanjali

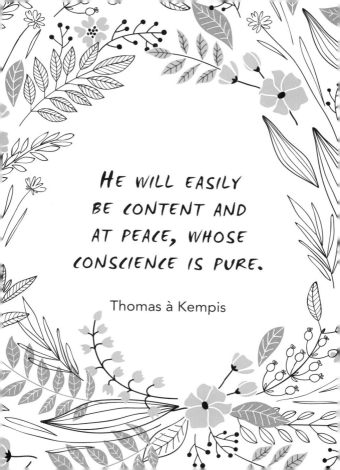

He will easily
be content and
at peace, whose
conscience is pure.

Thomas à Kempis

By time and toil,
we accomplish more
than strength or
rage ever could.

Jean de la Fontaine

There is no
way to peace; peace
is the way.

A. J. Muste

In control of desires
stillness is attained.
In stillness the
world is restored.

Lao Tzu

Everything comes
GRADUALLY
and at its
APPOINTED HOUR.

Ovid

Quiet minds
cannot be perplexed
or frightened, but
go on in fortune or
misfortune at their
own private pace,
like a clock during
a thunderstorm.

Robert Louis Stevenson

PEACE IS NOT
AN ABSENCE
OF WAR; IT
IS A VIRTUE,
A STATE
OF MIND...
CONFIDENCE,
JUSTICE.

Baruch Spinoza

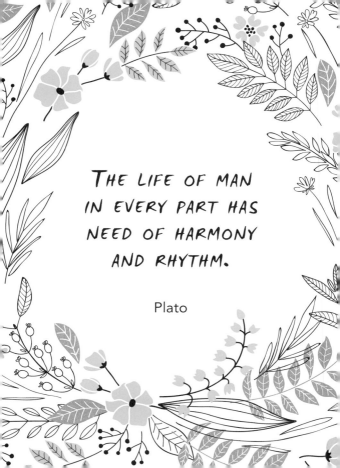

THE LIFE OF MAN
IN EVERY PART HAS
NEED OF HARMONY
AND RHYTHM.

Plato

If the
INNER MIND
has been tamed, the
OUTER ENEMY
cannot harm you.

Atīśa

If a man wishes to
be sure of the road
he treads on, he must
close his eyes and
walk in the dark.

St John of the Cross

A MAN OF
MEDITATION
IS HAPPY, NOT
FOR AN HOUR
A DAY, BUT
QUITE ROUND
THE CIRCLE OF
ALL HIS YEARS.

Isaac Taylor

The pursuit, even of the best things, ought to be calm and tranquil.

Cicero

THERE IS NO
GREATNESS WHERE
THERE IS NOT
SIMPLICITY.

Leo Tolstoy

Cheerfulness keeps up
a kind of daylight in
the mind, and fills
it with a steady and
perpetual serenity.

Joseph Addison

Do not let
trifles disturb your
tranquillity of mind.

Grenville Kleiser

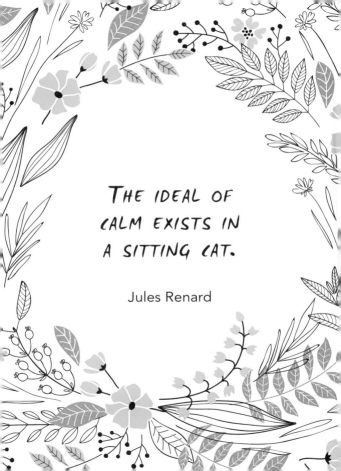

THE IDEAL OF
CALM EXISTS IN
A SITTING CAT.

Jules Renard

A PEACEFUL
MAN DOES
MORE GOOD
THAN A
LEARNED
ONE.

Pope John XXIII

Calmness is the
cradle of power.

J. G. Holland

WITHIN YOU
THERE IS A
STILLNESS AND
A SANCTUARY
TO WHICH YOU
CAN RETREAT AT
ANY TIME AND
BE YOURSELF.

Hermann Hesse

The Span of Life
is too short to
be trifled away in
unconcerning and
unprofitable Matters.

Mary Astell

I AM NOT AFRAID
OF TOMORROW,
FOR I HAVE SEEN
YESTERDAY AND
I LOVE TODAY.

William Allen White

WORK, ALTERNATED
WITH NEEDFUL REST,
IS THE SALVATION OF
MAN OR WOMAN.

Antoinette Brown Blackwell

Power is so CHARACTERISTICALLY CALM, *that calmness in itself has the* ASPECT OF STRENGTH.

Edward Bulwer-Lytton

FORGET THE
PAST AND LIVE THE
PRESENT HOUR.

Sarah Knowles Bolton

ONE'S ACTION
OUGHT TO
COME OUT OF
AN ACHIEVED
STILLNESS:
NOT BE
A MERE
RUSHING ON.

D. H. Lawrence

LEARN TO BE
CALM AND
YOU WILL
ALWAYS BE
HAPPY.

Paramahansa Yogananda

One often calms
one's grief by
recounting it.

Pierre Corneille

Every now and then go
away, have a little
relaxation, for when
you come back to your
work your judgement
will be surer.

Leonardo da Vinci

HE THAT
CAN HAVE
PATIENCE CAN
HAVE WHAT
HE WILL.

Benjamin Franklin

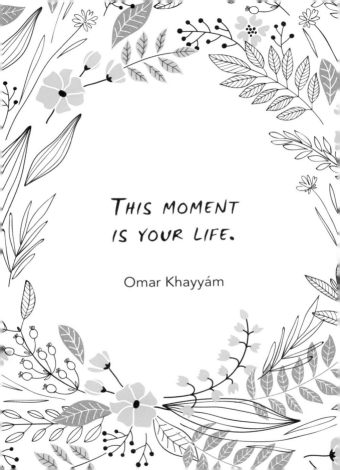

THIS MOMENT
IS YOUR LIFE.

Omar Khayyám

Change your
thoughts and you
change your world.

Norman Vincent Peale

Peace is its own reward.

Mahatma Gandhi

There are always
flowers for
those who want
to see them.

Henri Matisse

YOU NEED NOT WRESTLE FOR YOUR GOOD. YOUR GOOD FLOWS TO YOU MOST EASILY WHEN YOU ARE RELAXED, OPEN AND TRUSTING.

Alan Cohen

YOU CANNOT SHAKE
HANDS WITH A
CLENCHED FIST.

Indira Gandhi

We must let go of
the life we have
planned, so as to
accept the one that
is waiting for us.

Joseph Campbell

Nothing is
worth more than
this day.

Johann Wolfgang
von Goethe

You will never find time for anything. If you want the time, you must make it.

Charles Buxton

He who angers you

CONQUERS YOU.

Elizabeth Kenny

The more tranquil
a man becomes,
the greater is
his success, his
influence, his power
for good.

James Allen

GOOD HUMOUR
IS A TONIC
FOR MIND AND
BODY... IT IS
THE DIRECT
ROUTE TO
SERENITY AND
CONTENTMENT.

Grenville Kleiser

SET PEACE
OF MIND
AS YOUR
HIGHEST
GOAL, AND
ORGANISE
YOUR LIFE
AROUND IT.

Brian Tracey

I will be calm.
I will be
the mistress
of myself.

Jane Austen

He who lives in
harmony with himself
lives in harmony with
the world.

Marcus Aurelius

WHEN ONE DOOR OF
HAPPINESS CLOSES,
ANOTHER OPENS.

Helen Keller

If you're interested in finding out more about our books, find us on Facebook at Summersdale Publishers and follow us on Twitter at @Summersdale.

www.summersdale.com

Image credits

G000162434

By the same author:

Living Holiness
Living Faith
Living Sacrifice

Living Stones

Seventy-five Years of WEC International

Helen M. Roseveare

HODDER AND STOUGHTON
LONDON   SYDNEY   AUCKLAND   TORONTO

British Library Cataloguing in Publication Data

Roseveare, Helen, M.,
    Living stones: seventy-five years
    of WEC International.—(Hodder
Christian paperbacks).
    1. WEC International—History
I. Title
269′.2′0601   BV3752.W6

ISBN 0-340-42462-1

As you come to Him, the LIVING STONE – rejected by men, but chosen by God and precious to Him – you also, like LIVING STONES, are being built into a spiritual house, to be a holy priesthood, offering spiritual sacrifices acceptable to God through Jesus Christ . . .

That you may declare the praises of Him who called you out of darkness into His wonderful light.

1 Pet. 2:4–9.

You are worthy to take the scroll
and to open its seals, because You were slain,
and with Your blood You
purchased men for God
from every tribe and language and
people and nation.
You have made them to be a kingdom
and priests to serve our God,
and they will reign on the earth.

Rev. 5:9–10.

After this I looked and there before me was a great multitude, that no one could count, from every nation, tribe, people and language, standing before the Throne and in front of the Lamb.

Rev. 7:9.

Contents

Foreword

Who said that mission work is dull and boring? Not if you read this gem of a book! Every chapter sparkles with the light of heaven. Your heart will be thrilled and your faith strengthened as you read.

In *Living Stones* Helen has given WEC (Worldwide Evangelization Crusade) a fitting seventy-fifth birthday present. The Lord Jesus is uplifted in this wide variety of testimonies, deliverances, demonstrations of the power of God, and breakthroughs for the gospel. Problems, difficulties and sufferings abound in today's world, and the Christian life is a battle with not a few personal defeats – but these are not the subject of this book. Why add to the prevalent negativism? God reigns indeed, so may this book glorify Him through what He is doing!

Here Helen has written a fitting sequel to her series of "Living" books that have been so widely read and appreciated. Each book covers one of WEC's four foundational principles, or "Four Pillars": Sacrifice, Faith, Holiness and (to follow) Fellowship. Here she has drawn all four together in short chapters which cover the seventy-five years of WEC history. They can only be representative of the work of 3,000 or more past and present Weccers labouring in over fifty countries on six continents. They movingly encapsulate that history in a most readable form.

The Lord gave us a new challenge in 1984 – over 120 specific goals – to unreached peoples, unevangelised cities and unoccupied regions around the world. By 1987 about seventy of these had been initiated. More stories of the triumphs of the gospel are in the making. Yet there remains much land to be possessed!

We want Jesus back again! Only sacrificial obedience will hasten His return. May *Living Stones* help you to play your part. We need volunteers NOW – prayer warriors, witnesses, long term missionaries of every kind. Are you one of them? It may be dangerous for you to read on, for God may speak to you about your part in evangelising the world.

Patrick J. Johnstone
Deputy International Secretary
WEC International
Bulstrode
Gerrards Cross
Bucks SL9 8SZ
England

Introduction

WEC International, an interdenominational evangelical missionary society, known for many years as the World-wide Evangelization Crusade, was born in 1913, through the vision and obedience of one man, C. T. Studd. The mission is seventy-five years old in 1988. This book has been written to mark this milestone in her history; but as one of her leaders has remarked: "Milestones are for passing, not for sitting on!"

WEC International acknowledged, from its inception, GOD alone, Father, Son and Spirit, to be its Founder, Establisher and Commander. Jesus Christ, and the vital necessity of His Cross and substitutionary death for the redemption of all mankind, is the basis of all the mission's activities. The mission believes that all believers are called of God to aid in taking the message of reconciliation to the uttermost parts of the earth in each succeeding generation.

WEC was built on "four pillars" considered essential for the fulfilment of its commission, "to evangelise the remaining unevangelised peoples of the earth" as speedily as possible – SACRIFICE, FAITH, HOLINESS and FELLOWSHIP. Without a willingness for supreme sacrifice, without humility to accept God's resources by faith, without a deep desire for Christlikeness in daily living, and without a total abandonment to self-denial and fellowship with all other believers, the task cannot be achieved.

The following stories have been selected from each of the seventy-five years of the mission's history to illustrate her growth – from one man in one place, to over twelve hundred full-time missionaries and countless national pastors and workers in more than forty countries around the world. At the same time, the stories were found to illustrate the four pillars, broadly speaking in four periods of time, though with much inevitable overlapping. The first nineteen years were especially marked by sacrifice (though in no wise lacking in faith and holiness); the second period developed supremely around the faith principle (though sacrifice and holiness were equally part of the whole); holiness became the paramount need during the third period; and fellowship is undoubtedly the special hallmark of the present time.

The collator of these accounts trusts that the biblical principles and teaching on mission, though not spelt out as such, will be apparent through the testimonies. Should they enthuse others to join the ranks of full-time cross-cultural missionary workers in whatever organisation, one of the objects of the writing will have been achieved. Though basically the book reveals the story of the growth of WEC International, the reader can ignore the label and enjoy and be challenged by the content.

Inevitably, seventy-five short chapters in story form can only scratch the surface, and this book does not seek to be a history. Justice cannot be done to the people involved, the tasks undertaken, the sacrifices made, the cost willingly accepted and often endured. Much has obviously had to be omitted, and no effort has been made to record all the mistakes and failures, as would have been necessary in a specifically historical record. Though not claiming to be a history, it is all nevertheless historically true.

We do not wish to glorify men, nor to blow our own trumpet, nor to rest on our laurels, but rather to give glory to God for what has been achieved; to express our gratitude and give encouragement to those who have so faithfully prayed for such achievements; and to challenge others to join the ranks to help us all "pass more milestones".

So may these testimonies stir our imagination and fire our hearts into obedience to Christ's last command: "You shall be My witnesses in Jerusalem, and in all Judea and Samaria, and to the ends of the earth" (Acts 1:8). Then, together, we shall go forward to "evangelise the remaining unevangelised peoples in the shortest possible time" so as to hasten the return of our Lord and Saviour as King and Judge of all the earth.

Prologue

THE TRAIL BLAZER

Broken in health and uncertain as to his future, a middle-aged man walked along a street in Liverpool in 1908. Little did he suspect that a seed sown into his heart that afternoon would germinate into a giant movement, thousands of thousands strong, encircling the world.

Arrested by a curiously worded notice outside a meeting hall, CANNIBALS WANT MISSIONARIES, C. T. Studd went in to hear a message that was to change the course of his life. To a crowded audience, Dr Karl Kumm, an intrepid explorer, was giving a vivid report of his travels across the great continent of Africa. He commented that numberless tribes were being exploited by big-game hunters and cruel slave-traders, and yet had never heard the story of Jesus Christ.

Studd was shaken to the core by Kumm's challenge. That no one had cared enough to take the gospel to these people, even though so many were willing to dare all for personal gain, filled his heart with shame. He became immediately and irrevocably involved on their behalf. The knowledge that he was a sick man and without financial backing did not deter him. The suspicion that no one might be willing to sponsor him, and the obvious fact that no one else in the meeting was willing to respond to the challenge, only intensified his resolve.

Charlie Studd (or C. T. as he has become known to thousands) was not one to back out when hemmed in with difficulties. As a university student, he had already thrown away a promising career as an athlete, when he surrendered his life to Christ. Under the dynamic leadership of Hudson Taylor in China, he had given away his not-inconsiderable fortune, inherited from his father, in order to be free from such "a bothersome encumbrance", in his service for his Master. So was he not now prepared to sacrifice his very life, if need be, that Christ's love might reach those unreached tribesmen in the dark heart of Africa?

"Gentlemen," Studd declared a few months later, to the members of a would-be committee, who had just refused to back his project: "God has called me to go, and so go I must." As they drew his attention to the doctor's verdict that such a trip to Africa must send him to his grave, he exclaimed, with characteristic impatient zeal, "I will blaze the trail, even though my grave become a stepping stone, that younger men may follow."

In 1910, he sailed from Liverpool for Africa, to investigate the needs of the southern Sudan and to ascertain the strength of the southward-advancing forces of Islam.

The first night on board ship, God spoke to him, declaring: "This trip is not merely for the Sudan: it is for *the whole unevangelised world*!" and his imagination was fired by the breadth of the vision. "God speaks to me of a new Crusade," he wrote to his wife. "It burns in my brain and heart."

Journeying south from Khartoum, by boat and on mule, consumed with a passion to reach people with the good news of the gospel, he heard of vast numbers of people, yet further south in the Congo, depraved and destitute, who also had never heard of Jesus Christ.

"Dare you," God challenged Studd, as he returned north, down the Nile, "dare you go back to spend the remainder of your days in England, knowing of these masses who have never yet heard of My Son?" That settled it for C. T. He hadn't the will to stay in England with such a call in his heart!

Arriving home, he challenged all he met with the needs of the unevangelised world. He wrote stirring appeals, that burned with the passion of Christ for the lost. In 1913, he outlined the principles of a new Crusade, calling its members "Christ's etceteras" and acknowledging as its director the Triune God alone. Its purpose was to reach out beyond the furthest reach of all other missionary forces, as a "supplementary worldwide evangelisation society", that would take neither personnel nor money from existing works.

"Our method", he declared, "is to search and find out what parts of the world at present remain unevangelised, and then by faith in Christ, by prayer to God, by obedience to the Holy Ghost, by courage, determination and supreme sacrifice, to accomplish their evangelisation with the utmost despatch.

"Too long have we been waiting for another to begin," he cried. "The time for waiting is past! The hour of God has struck! War is declared! In God's holy Name, let us arise and build!"

So it was that one man, in one place, heard a call from God and caught a fresh vision of the dying souls of men.

"If Jesus Christ be God, and died for me, then no sacrifice can be too great for me to make for Him!" he cried aloud for all to hear: and from that tiny, apparently insignificant, source began a trickle that was to become a mighty river to reach out through the sacrificial lives of thousands of men and women, in over forty countries around the world, to bring the Water of Life to countless multitudes of those who were, seventy-five years ago, the "unreached and unevangelised".

Part One

SACRIFICE

1913–1931

"Christianity is based on *sacrifice*." So wrote young Jack Harrison, the truth having been burned into his heart through eight years of working closely alongside his fiery leader, C. T. Studd. "Take away sacrifice, and what is left? An insipid lifeless nothing, a shell without the explosive cordite; a bunghole without a barrel; a farce, not a force. Sacrifice is written large over the pages of Holy Writ – God so loved that He gave Heaven's best. Jesus so loved that He laid down His life. Unto us His followers it is given, on His behalf, not only to believe but also to suffer for His sake."

"There is no gain but by a loss"

There is no gain but by a loss,
   We cannot save but by the Cross;
The corn of wheat to multiply,
   Must fall into the ground and die.
O, should a soul alone remain
When it a hundredfold can gain?

Our souls are held by all they hold;
   Slaves still are slaves in chains of gold:
To whatsoever we may cling,
   We make it a soul-chaining thing,
Whether it be a life or land,
And dear as our right eye or hand.

Whenever you ripe fields behold,
   Waving to God their sheaves of gold,
Be sure some corn of wheat has died,
   Some saintly soul been crucified:
Someone has suffered, wept and prayed,
And fought hell's legions undismayed!

A. S. Booth-Clibborn

1913 – A "dainty" companion

A school report from Repton on young Alfred Buxton stated that he was considered "to be a little dainty"!

However, when, as a third year medical student, Alfred had heard and been fired by the enthusiasm of the same Dr Kumm, who had challenged the heart of Studd, there was nothing particularly "dainty" about his response!

When advised on all sides that he was not strong enough, physically or spiritually, to accompany C. T., the rugged pioneer, on his "mad-cap, ill-conceived foray" into Africa, iron had entered Alfred's soul.

"I've counted the cost," he wrote to his father: "and God has clearly given me my marching orders to set forth."

He was in love with one of C. T.'s daughters, Edith, but at that time she did not seem interested in him. He counted the cost, and prepared to go without her.

He was a medical student, with a good career ahead of him and secure prospects, but God's voice had said, "Do thy diligence to come quickly!" He counted the cost, and prepared to go without the coveted degree.

He was the son of devoted missionary parents, who felt he was too young and inexperienced for the task to be undertaken, but God said: "Go in this thy might." He counted the cost, and prepared to go, even without the longed-for parental blessing.

Then God had stepped in!

At his valedictory service, Edith suddenly saw him with new eyes, and knew that to remain at home without him would be unbearable. He remained after all to obtain his B.A. degree with honours, but lost his interest in medicine. His father accepted God's will, and even rejoiced that his son was going out in obedience to the clear command of the King of kings.

So it was that C. T. Studd arrived in Africa in 1913 and eventually, with Alfred Buxton, headed for the Belgian Congo. Together they journeyed through Kenya and Uganda. Together they battled through severe attacks of malarial fever and various other dangers to life in the tropics. Together they stood firm to God's call through every endeavour to deter them. God's promise that they should be "more-than-conquerors" spurred them on over and over again!

"So at last they had gained their hearts' desire," wrote their biographer, as, after nine months' arduous travelling, they reached Niangara in Zaïre, the very heart of Africa. There, in the northern fringes of the great Ituri rain-forest, they set up, for the exorbitant sum of six pounds, their first "home" which they impishly nick-named "Buckingham Palace"!

As he continued "to count the cost", Alfred wrote home that he was not so sure what the price was that he was being asked to pay! "It is all so civilised and different from what I expected," he exclaimed. "We hardly miss European stuff at all! It is strange how little you really need when the pinch comes" – a box for clothes and books, a suitcase for a few extras, a sack for bedding. "We live on a verandah, with two rooms as store-houses," he explained, "a real palace! Having food and raiment we are therewith content." So wrote the "dainty" warrior!

Alfred gave himself to the study of Bangala, the *lingua franca*, putting together a dictionary of some 2,500 words. He started the translation of Mark's Gospel, in between the numerous trips in all directions to spy out their new land.

After five days' trek to the south, along palm-lined forest paths, they came to Nala, in the midst of the pigmy people, and found themselves surrounded by tribes: Azandes and Mangbetus, Medjes and Mayagos, in one of the most densely populated areas of Congo.

Five more long days brought them to Pawa, Ibambi and Wamba, amidst dense crowds of Wabudu tribesmen. On again northwards to Poko, and everywhere *people*, waiting to hear the good news, that there was a "way back to God from the dark paths of sin", and that Jesus had died "that they might be forgiven." Back to Niangara, and off again by canoe down river for six days, westwards to reach Bambili.

"The memory of these long treks," Buxton wrote later, "conjures up the picture of a dark, chilly morning; a hasty breakfast off the remains of supper; the quick rolling up of bedding and adjusting the loads; the short prayer, followed by the shouts and whoops of the porters, disappearing along the narrow winding path, drenched in dew; tramping through scorching midday heat, until we arrived at a village. Always an excited welcome, and then the invitation by the chieftain to share the reason for our visit."

"In spiritually overfed England," Alfred recalled, "one must usually do much advertising to get a congregation. Here, wherever you go, you find an audience clamouring to be taught! It is a solemn fact", he concluded, "that though we have travelled eleven days to the south and ten days to the west, probably none of the masses of people whom we have met have ever before seen the face or heard the voice of a Protestant missionary!"

1914 – Ox-cart and all

"Oh, no!"

Irene Flangham's startled cry rent the night quiet, as she felt herself being hurtled through the air and deposited untidily in a heap at the side of the rough dirt-track road.

The two men, walking slightly ahead of the ox-drawn cart, hurried back to the aid of the three ladies, who were struggling to their feet. Together they looked with dismay at the broken-down wagon and all their property, scattered in every direction across the narrow road.

It seemed the last straw. They were all tired, having set out at six that morning. They had been on the road ever since, and now it was almost 9 p.m. The other two members of their party had cycled on ahead to find accommodation for the night at the next village.

It was sixty days since the party had made their farewells at Fenchurch Street Station in London to begin their three month trek to Niangara in north-east Congo. Two weeks by ocean steamer had brought them to Port Said. A short train journey to Cairo had followed, and then three weeks of crowded, noisy sailing up the Nile by river boat. From Rejaf, they had started this last three hundred mile lap of their journey to Niangara, walking and cycling by the side of the laden ox-drawn wagon. When dark had dropped upon them that evening, the three ladies gratefully accepted the suggestion that they should clamber on the cart, and sit atop their baggage until they reached the guest house at the next village.

And disaster struck!

Meanwhile, at Niangara, tremendous preparations were afoot to welcome this first group of reinforcements. Temporary buildings were being erected; seven acres of bush land cultivated; a well dug.

Elsewhere, the work continued to grow apace. At Nala, three days' trek to the south, chiefs had signed over a good concession to the missionaries, attaching their thumb prints to the legal document. A brick building was erected, and C. T. promised the villagers a hospital and an industrial school, as soon as suitable personnel became available.

In Medje territory, four days' trek to the west, where ten years before a white man, sent to subdue the tribe with thirty-five soldiers, had been killed, cooked and eaten, the missionaries were now well received.

At Chief Okondo's village, the great man himself had received them. After much dancing by his numerous wives, he called for silence, and Alfred Buxton rose and spoke. Never before had Okondo and his people heard the gospel.

Darkness fell, lit up by occasional flashes of lightning. When at last the crowd scattered, they demanded another service the next day! An even bigger crowd gathered, and "drew nearer, to hear better". Buxton had another opportunity that anyone might envy. "When we finally arose", C. T. wrote, "the whole audience gave a great shout and swarmed around us!"

In his letters to his father, however, Alfred reveals an ever-deepening yearning in his soul. He had discovered that enthusiasm and consecration were insufficient to achieve the task to which God had called him. Service for Christ, obedience to Christ, witness for Christ – these could not of themselves satisfy the growing hunger in his heart. He was going through the travail of self-revelation, self-stripping, self-emptying, which every soldier in Christ's army has to learn, that he might know the wonderful release of the truth contained in Paul's great acclamation: "I have been crucified with Christ and I no longer live: but Christ lives in me."

The wagon was eventually repaired and the party of reinforcements pushed on. "Through fair weather and foul, through health and sickness, the good hand of our God has been with us," wrote their leader.

As they approached Niangara, neat and clean villages, half hidden in banana groves, became more numerous. The party's excitement rose. At last, eighty-two days after leaving London, the party walked into Niangara to a rapturous welcome. "Whether the folk understand our mission or not", wrote one of the new party, "they have given us a hearty welcome, making us feel at home in a strange land. We do indeed praise our heavenly Father for the protecting care of these many weeks, bringing us in health and strength to our desired haven."

It was just one week to Christmas, and the hearts of the eight missionaries were filled with praise.

"Though I have left you all", wrote Irene Flangham to

her family at home, on that first Christmas eve that she spent in the Congo, "I can truly say, I would not change my place with anyone whatever their position was. I am so sure this, and only this, is His place for me!"

1915 – By love compelled

Leaving Alfred Buxton in charge of the growing family of missionaries, C. T. returned to his wife and daughters in England, to see how well the young mission was now established at the home base. He toured extensively and marvelled at the many praying groups and at the spirit of sacrifice amongst their members. Everywhere he went, he poured his heart out, challenging young folk to "move out for God". Many responded.

His advice to those offering for "the front" was often unorthodox and even disconcerting.

"Read and prepare practically," he stressed. "Learn to cook, to garden, to carpenter, to sew, to put up a simple house, to be a handyman, to get your shins kicked and have a sore head without thinking it necessary to 'lose your wool'. Above all, read your Bible. It is not biblical lollipops that are of use out there; but good healthy cuts off the joint of God's Word. Do not wait too long; the battlefield is the best training ground for a soldier. The great question is whether you have been chosen of God for so great an honour and privilege. You should ask Him if you *may* come. Never ask Him 'Must I go?' or He will surely say 'No!' and not change His mind!"

C. T.'s wife, Priscilla, had done a marvellous job. Too ill to accompany her husband on his first trip to the Congo, and concerned for the welfare of their four growing daughters, she had not at first been exactly keen about C. T. setting out once again to some benighted mission-field. He was already in his fifties, and broken in health, eaten up with asthma and racked with stomach pains. It just hadn't seemed reasonable to her. But his enthusiasm and his certainty of God's call had eventually broken down all her defences, and God had filled her with the same worldwide vision that had caught her husband's imagination. She had rallied from her sick bed, and become the infant mission's most ardent worker and advocate.

Now while the two of them were enjoying being and working together again, news trickled home from the "front" and filled their hearts with praise. Twelve had publicly declared their faith at Niangara, and eighteen at Nala!

"How could God do such things with such poor tools?" queried C. T. Studd. He went on to explain what was in his mind: "God made and chose another ruddy stripling as David of old – no regular warrior, just a simple lad and unordained of men – considered 'too young, too weak, too inexperienced' by many. 'Dainty!' But God has made this boy a linguist, poet, preacher, scribe and translator of His Word!"

This same "stripling", Alfred Buxton, wrote thrilling reports home of all that God was doing. Niangara, Nala, and now Bambili had been "occupied". At each centre, "camp followers" were crowding in to help put up necessary buildings and to learn to read. Hymns were being written and the book of Psalms translated. Schools were being started.

"As for recruits from home", he wrote, "send us people with initiative, who can carry themselves and others too. Such as need to be carried hamper the work. If any have jealousy, pride or tale-bearing traits lurking about them, do not send them, nor any who are prone to criticise. Send only Pauls and Timothys; men who are full of zeal, holiness and power. All others are hindrances.

"At Niangara", he continued, "things are going with a hum! The Misses Chapman and Flangham have daily classes, and all the meetings are better attended than last year. All the baptised converts are going strong, having evidently learned the secret that those who water others are themselves watered from above!"

Alfred had completed the translation of Mark's Gospel, and every morning the ladies were teaching some thirty to forty men and women to read it. "It is so exciting to see changed lives as God's Word enters their hearts. At every opportunity, the gospel is preached. Some of the local believers, living in utter darkness only two years previously and as yet with no Bible, are becoming fiery preachers!"

"How do you remember so well what we have taught you?" Irene asked them.

"After I have heard God's Word," one answered, "I go to my hut and pray God to hide His Word in my heart!"

To the south at Nala, the spiritual work was progressing and several more were being prepared for baptism. "Eighteen were baptised here on October 27th," Mr Coles wrote enthusiastically. "The Holy Spirit is mightily moving among the people, setting them free with a wonderful deliverance."

To the west, at Bambili, the Richardsons were digging in and God was blessing there too. All this work was not without opposition. Other white men in the area, afraid of losing their power over the local people, told the villagers not to give water to the missionaries, nor to direct them if lost in the jungle.

However, despite these threats of dire consequences, when the Richardsons told the chieftain that they wanted to hold an open-air service in his village to tell his people "the things of the great God", he brought together a huge congregation, sending his soldiers in all directions to bring in workmen as they returned home to their villages, and then herding in the prisoners from the local jail to swell the audience! Truly it was a case of "Go into the highways and byways, and compel them to come in!" and God worked in their hearts in a remarkable way, many accepting Christ as their personal Saviour and coming into the joy of true forgiveness of their sins.

1916 – Mounting excitement

"What has not God done for us?" was the triumphant opening sentence in the January magazine in 1916, only three years after the birth of the Heart of Africa Mission.

On July 14th, 1916, there was a great day of prayer and praise at the Central Hall, Westminster, when the new mission was officially named and dedicated.

A party of nine recruits, along with C. T. Studd himself, were bade farewell. Travelling from London to Kinshasa by steamer, they then chugged 700 miles up-river in a slow-moving barge. The final 300 miles was on foot through virgin forest, northwards to Nala – and what a reception awaited them there!

Seven more sailed in November and excitement mounted! The "two" of 1913 became "twenty-two" before 1916 was out. The "one" centre at Niangara became fourteen manned outposts.

Throughout the year, news flowed home of all that God was doing at and around Niangara, Nala, Poko and Bambili. Throughout the year, challenges flowed from the pen of the Studds to Christians in and around the United Kingdom.

From Niangara, Irene Flangham told of the building of the new church, including waiting-room, class-room, dispensary and vestry! The first church elders had been trained and appointed, and "it is thrilling to see them leading services and giving testimonies." Little did they then realise that one of these, Boimi, was to become an elder statesman of the Church throughout the central north-eastern province of the Belgian Congo in later years.

C. T. wrote: "Whatever you've got, use it for God, and don't wait for what you've not got! If you've only a donkey's jaw-bone, bray for all you're worth! A braying ass has been known to talk more sense than a prophet!"

From Nala came exciting news of Gemisi, only six months a Christian, newly baptised, who had taken charge of the centre. When some of the baptised Christians began to falter and return to their fetishes, he exhorted them to remain true to God. When some of the church members had been very ill and without medical help, he prayed for them and saw God heal them. When some of the surrounding chieftains began to be hostile, he had visited them and preached the Word to them. As a result, these same chiefs were now sending their sons to the school, to learn to read! Furthermore, Gemisi had thoroughly prepared thirteen men and twelve women for baptism.

C. T. Studd wrote: "Don't you remember how Hudson Taylor received his commission for inland China? He verily believed that the Lord had been searching throughout the length and breadth of the land to find someone ignorant enough, weak enough and humble enough that He Himself could use, and who would give Him the glory, and that then He hit upon him (Hudson Taylor) and said: 'This man will do! He has all the requirements; he is ignorant, weak and helpless enough, so I can use him.' These are the only three degrees absolutely necessary to the man of God!"

From Bambili, the Richardsons told of the establishing of the work to the south of the river, among the Ababua people. Not only had a church building been erected, but several lads had been saved, and were now themselves preaching the gospel to others. The work among the Azandes, to the north of the river, was much harder, yet there too they witnessed "God's almighty hand changing the hearts of greedy, lazy, thoughtless lads, the offspring of cannibals, into children of God!" Their main prayer was: "Send us more workers!"

A British Army officer, summing up neatly what sort of "more workers" were needed, wrote: "Unless you have missionaries so full of the Spirit of Christ that they count not their own lives dear to them, you will probably look in vain for converts who will be prepared to lose their lives in the Master's service. It is supremely important to have the right stamp of men – men who have made some sacrifice yet count it as privilege and honour: men who do not know what discouragement means, and who expect great things from God. Such men are not manufactured: they are God-made. The Master who has need of them is able to provide them." And he ended by saying: "Missions mean warfare. Should the soldiers of the Cross shrink from undertaking on behalf of Christ what is being done every day for commerce or conquest?"

1917 – Shattering contrasts

Black wedding, white wedding.

Little Fulani, who came to live at Nala, had no hands. When still a child, she had been sold to a disagreeable old man, ill-kept and dirty. The money was needed to pay dowry for her older brother's wedding to the same old man's daughter! The child became the slave of the older wives, and at everyone's beck and call. Unable to abide the horror of her filthy husband, she ran away, not once but twice. After she had been found and returned to the cruel man the second time, he tied her wrists tightly together, hung her up in a tree for two nights and whipped her savagely. Her hands dropped off. Such was the lot of women.

Edith Studd arrived at Nala with her father, in November 1916. Travelling up country by slow river barge, she waited impatiently for the first sign of shore at Kisangani, where "her white man" should be waiting for her. Four long years had passed since they were last together.

"There he is – the one with the beard!"

It was the same voice and the same boy, but there was a little difference, "a difference that made him all the dearer to me!" Edith went on: "How proud I was of him, his battered hat, his shabby coat and worn sleeves." On the long three months' trek to Nala, they walked and talked, and caught up on their love for each other.

"It is my wedding morning," Edith wrote home on December 27th, 1916. "We had a service in our little mission first, and the Africans crowded in. In the middle of the service, an overloaded bench snapped in two, and with muffled cries, thirty Africans were shot onto the floor. I caught father's eye and nearly laughed!"

Then the official wedding ceremony, a great deal of bowing and scraping, and signing of papers "and all was over". It was the first white wedding ever performed in the heart of Africa. "The Commissioner was very nervous, but afterwards entertained us all to a wonderful dinner."

How different from the lot of poor little Fulani!

Another stark contrast can be drawn between the crude savagery of drunken men and the gentle bravery of un-daunted women. Nurse Arnall and Esme Roupell were out in the district trekking on one occasion, when they came to the compound of Chief Danga, a man who was seldom free from the influence of palm wine.

"The Chief said we could have a meeting," they wrote later. "We waited till nearly dark, but instead of keeping his promise he was having a merry time of wine drinking. So we took the bull by the horns and went into his audience hall. Though he was full of drink, we managed to quieten him, while lots of his people listened most earnestly to the gospel."

On another occasion, Edith Buxton and Irene Flangham had to flee in the night from Chief Kongoli who, in a drunken rage, stormed into their rest-house. "He wasn't still a minute, shouting and spitting. One minute he was angry, the next over-familiar. I have never experienced such awful moments in my life: it was like a nightmare. How we got out of that hellish hole I shall never know, except by God's help!"

But nothing daunted, these intrepid women crusaders stuck it out, and went back again and again, until a church had been established right in Chief Kongoli's compound!

When modern critics grumble that the white missionary has trampled on the national culture, they should ask the local people which they would prefer, white or black matrimonial methods, Christianity or witchcraft, sobriety or drunkenness – and they are not slow to give their response!

1918 – The great push – rain or no rain

"Storms usually burst in the afternoon," C. T. Studd wrote during the rainy season: "just about the time we hold our weekly market service; so we all prayed earnestly, and God has held off the storms in a truly remarkable fashion for five successive weeks!" They prayed away physical downpours, and prayed down spiritual ones instead! Every report of the year, from northern Niangara to southern Deti, from western Bambili to eastern Nala, was filled with rejoicing as God graciously poured out His Spirit upon the people.

Two women missionaries kept the work going at Niangara. Many converts were prepared for baptism. Thirty men were being trained to be evangelists. The children's school grew from strength to strength. A real fervour gripped everyone to preach the gospel "in season and out of season". Prayer meetings were crowded, everyone taking part. Two chieftains, who were coming regularly to the meetings, were under conviction of sin, and one of them had already burned all his witchcraft paraphernalia. Sick people crowded into the compound, coming great distances because they believed that the "God of the white ladies has power to heal us!"

At Poko, two Welshmen occupied the parcel of ground that the chief had given to the mission, which had lain empty for almost a year. In three weeks, they were able to visit all the chieftains in the region, representing some 30,000 men, women and children, and were well received everywhere. As all the people had to visit the Government Post annually to pay their taxes, they could "drop in" at the missionary home while there. This gave opportunity for the two missionaries to preach the gospel – on one occasion, several times daily for sixteen days – with wonderful effectiveness. Chiefs would sit on the verandah, drinking coffee, and drinking in the Word of God at the same time! All promised to build churches and schools: all demanded "teachers" – where will these be found?

"Oh, there is such need of a great push!" wrote Oscar Jenkins. "It is time for a great advance. We have been praying for open doors. Here are the open doors, and we cannot enter them! Cannot, did I say? We MUST. It is God's command, and He never commands a thing unless He knows it can and will be accomplished."

The push came, southwards into another hitherto un-reached region.

"The greatest advance of the year", wrote Alfred Buxton, "has without doubt been the opening of our first station in the Ituri district." On the top of Deti Hill, with a magnificent view in every direction, Mr and Mrs Ellis had opened a church centre, and once again, blessing was pouring down. There was a teeming population on all sides, and a good congregation gathered each Sunday, to listen to the gospel in "Kingwana", another trade-language.

God used so many varying situations to bring opportunities for the preaching of His Word. The birth of baby Samuel to the Richardsons at Bambili opened many doors: Africans love babies. The villagers clubbed together to see that the child had sufficient milk; and were then willing to hear the story of the birth of "God's Baby", sent into this world to save us.

The work at Kongoli grew, in the hands of those intrepid women workers, Esme Roupell and Nurse Arnall. "They deserve much credit", wrote Mr Coles, "for their labours of love. Whatever language they have been preaching in, it has been one through which the Holy Spirit was able to do a mighty work. It has not only tickled the ears of the Africans, but made their hearts to burn also. It is a wonderful thing to see and hear these so-called ignorant folks learning and singing hymns in such an outstanding fashion! It's a tonic to one's heart."

Wamba was occupied during the year by the Lowders,

and within a few months, they saw over one hundred converts, twenty of whom had been baptised.

At Nala, dispensary and hospital work so flourished that new and larger buildings were already required. Two hundred were attending adult school, with many candidates for baptism. The industrial school was growing apace, with enthusiastic classes in cane-chair making, shoe making and repairing, and tailoring and the use of a sewing machine. The boys' school had over one hundred attending, and marvel of marvels, the girls' school was also growing. Against all expectations, parents *had* sent their girls, and already there had been several Christian weddings!

1919 – Only need – endless pairs of boots

"The speediest possible fulfilment of the command of Christ to evangelise the *whole world* by a definite attempt to evangelise the remaining unevangelised parts of the earth."

On his journey to the Congo, C. T. Studd had written those words as the proposed objective of a new society, "a union mission – a supplementary worldwide evangelisation society," the latter word being changed to "crusade" shortly afterwards. The name Crusade caught the imagination of all the missionaries, "for that implies a fight, and a fight implies the need for courage, sacrifice and endurance!"

The first "definite attempt" to take the gospel to the "remaining unevangelised parts of the earth" was the entry into the heart of Africa. Here, the work had spread rapidly from Niangara to Ibambi, throughout the Welle district and into the Ituri district. Now, six years later, with an efficient home base in the United Kingdom and six church-centres occupied in Central Africa, the mission realised that God was directing them to begin work in other unevangelised parts.

However, during 1919, several missionaries had to return to England for needed rest and restoration of health.

In the Congo, the very small and depleted team were stretched to the limit. It seemed ludicrous at such a time to be speaking of an "advance" into other regions in the Welle and the Ituri, let alone into other countries in the world! Nevertheless, the mission put out extensive calls, to encourage and enthuse young men and women to "go forward for Christ!"

Under the able leadership of A. G. Barclay, son-in-law of C. T. Studd, a training centre had been opened in London to prepare men for missionary service. There was a hum of excitement in the air.

In the July magazine, there was a clarion call for candidates for pioneer work, and a declaration of intent made for a ten-fold increase in the mission's membership during 1919.

Things started to move. Early in the year, Norman Grubb and his newly-wedded wife Pauline (C. T. Studd's daughter) sailed, with Lilian Dennis, for Africa. In November, Leslie Sutton, Herbert Jenkinson and George Ambrose set out from Genoa to Alexandria en route for the Congo – and the number of missionaries in Africa started to grow again.

At the same time reports were coming in that fired the imagination of young men at home. James Lowder, a lean bearded man, with quite extraordinary stamina, who had helped to open up the work at Deti Hill, had moved four days to the south, to open up work in the Wamba region. Meetings were started there amongst the thousands who thronged the government market on Sundays, and God gave an abundant harvest.

James' appetite had been whetted, and he had set off on a seven month trip even further south, into as-yet unreached chieftains' villages. He was so fighting fit that he could cover prodigious distances every day, doing four normal "stages" in one, at a speed which would put anyone else on their back with fever! Pushing, splashing, climbing his way through some of the densest bush in the great Ituri forest taught him to reduce his travelling equipment to a bare minimum. He could sleep on anything, eat anything, endure anything. His only need was endless pairs of boots! Besides all of which, he was consumed by a burning desire to tell people of the love of God and His willingness to forgive their sins. Trekking on bicycle further and further southwards, he wrote of unbelievable opportunities and needs.

Letter after letter told of villages reached, the gospel preached, hundreds saved, tribesmen and pygmies alike giving their hearts to the Saviour. Witchcraft totems were burned: praying places were built. Over two thousand seven hundred professed conversion during this one trek alone. And every letter ended with such a remark as: "The need in all these places is for workers, both white and black. There is no one to leave behind to teach them: the work is crippled by this lack. Who will come and do this work?"

C. T. sent two of the newly arrived missionaries, George Ambrose and Sam Staniford, to join James. Any doubts that they had had that the work might be spurious or superficial were soon dispelled. "It is an amazing experience", Staniford wrote, "to see the wonderful work of God in these people. They are thirsty for the Word of God. What an honour to be called to such service!"

One is hardly surprised that the last Crusade magazine of the year carried a huge notice:

SITUATIONS VACANT!
Apply at once

For the Heart of Africa – WANTED
　　– fifty men and women who prefer a tough job to a soft one, and fighting for Jesus to sitting at home!
For the Heart of Asia and the Heart of Arabia – WANTED
　　– two men, strong in faith, courage and wisdom, to start the attack in each area!
For the Heart of South America – WANTED
　　– two similar men to go forthwith!

Nothing is guaranteed to any of the above in this life but hardships, difficulties and death, but in the world to come, honour and glory throughout eternity.

1920 – The enemy fights back

"Passing from one village to another", wrote George Ambrose from the Welle district, "everywhere people flocked round, desiring us to stop and tell them more of Christ. Many have built large churches at their own expense and came to plead with us to send them a teacher. Would to God the appeal of these unevangelised parts could be heard in the homeland! 'Ifs' and 'buts' would give place to a large army of stalwarts going forth in obedience to the Command of Christ!"

"One morning", wrote Lowder from the Ituri district, "I received a challenge from the Bili witch-doctor, saying I was afraid to visit his house as I knew it would mean my death. Such a challenge couldn't be allowed to pass, so off I went with an ex-witch-doctor and two evangelists." Praying for protection, they made their way along the endlessly winding path, cutting through the rough barriers of thorn bushes erected to keep them out, until they reached the gate of the village. As the Christians rushed in, the "doctors" scattered into the forest! Triumphantly they destroyed the "garden" with all its evidence of the evil work conducted there, and returned praising God for His protection. As a direct result, "the head of that Bili house and a large following, including several witch-doctors, came to hear the gospel, listening attentively to the good news of salvation through the blood of Jesus."

At the same time as these reports of blessing were flooding in, the devil was sowing dissension among the workers, opposing the preaching of the gospel at every turn. Surrounded as they were by such obvious needs and endless opportunities, C. T. was torn apart to realise that all was not well within the missionary team.

A few were opposed to his strong emphasis on the absolute necessity of practical holiness in the lives of all believers. A few were not willing for a life of naked faith and supreme sacrifice, if this meant living rough and eating plain, with no holidays or recreations but just complete absorption in the one task of taking the gospel to the unreached. A few disliked his dictatorial methods of leadership, which finally led to the dismissal of two workers and the consequent resignation of several others.

When challenged about these things, C. T. was unrepentant.

"While here in the saddle," he wrote, "I intend to ride and to get others to ride, and not to be carried to heaven on flowery beds of ease. God teaches us not merely to endure sacrifices, but to suffer them with joy and to crave for more."

In the midst of all the turmoil, C. T. "received orders" from home to take a furlough, as they had heard of his great weakness and bouts of severe recurring pain, as well as rumours of the discontent among certain members of the team.

"What?" he cried. "You ask, you plead, you almost command me to come home, as soon as Alfred and Edith get back here? *But such cannot be* till there are sufficient reinforcements to hold and turn the battle in the gate."

There was a desperate need for someone to take the gospel south to the Wabari people, where stood a wide-open door. Even though it meant learning yet another language, Studd was willing to go himself rather than leave them without a missionary. "If deafness, age and failing sight render the speaking with even a halting and stammering tongue an impossibility," he continued, without the slightest trace of self-pity or complaint, "I still could pray!"

"As others will not venture a single innings against the devil's fast bowling in this fiery pitch," he concluded his letter, "just put down my name for a follow-on!"

Days of fierce conflict followed, even some of the home-committee questioning his decisions. C. T.'s uncompromising refusal to parley with those who wanted changes, his refusal to come home unless God specifically ordered him to do so, his indifference to the opinions of men and yet his unswerving loyalty to the first principles of the Crusade, caused a turbulence among the missionaries and eventually divided them into two camps.

The experience was a Gethsemane to C. T. Every now and again his letters to his wife betrayed something of what all this cost him: "Sometimes I feel that my Cross is heavy beyond endurance, and I fear I often feel like fainting under it. My heart seems worn out and bruised beyond repair, and in my deep loneliness I often wish to be gone. But God knows best, and I want to do every ounce of work He wants me to do."

1921 – Manufacturing soldiers

"Remember", Booth-Tucker had written to C. T. Studd when he was still in China, "that mere soul-saving is comparatively easy work, and is not nearly so important as that of manufacturing the saved ones into saints, soldiers and saviours."

This challenge now faced the WEC missionaries as dark clouds were gathering over the infant Church.

At Nala, following the initial years of growth, there came disappointments. Some Christians were lured away from church work with its nominal wages, by the promise of better wages from government employment. Slothfulness and self-seeking appeared, even among some of the evangelists. Others fell into moral sin and had to be dismissed.

At Poko, the whole team of twenty evangelists "struck" for more pay. Some of the most reliable leaders fell away. It came as a rude awakening for the missionaries.

At and around Ibambi, laziness and a lack of love began

to show themselves. The people would sing of love and talk about it, "but when it comes to sacrificing or working for God, their love becomes a ghost!" There was no sense of fear in the presence of a holy God. Converted, baptised and on their way to heaven, it no longer mattered to many of them that they lied, deceived, stole and committed adultery.

C. T. Studd had never been satisfied with a shallow work. His heart yearned to see a holy Church made up of Christians who knew, not only that their past sins were forgiven, but also that their present lives were empowered by the Spirit, so that they might be pleasing to God.

"It is all very well", he wrote, "to sing hymns and go to worship, but what we must see are the fruits of the Spirit and a really changed life and heart, a hatred of sin and a passion for righteousness. God can do it, and we must be content with nothing less."

The missionaries had to meet the challenge head on. Were they going to be content with half-hearted, shoddy Christianity, or were they willing to struggle, "travailing again in birth" to see Christ formed in each convert?

If there was to be a Church after the New Testament pattern, pleasing to God, "without spot or blemish," sanctification had to be added to justification. It was not that this had not been taught. It had. But the second stage of the battle, to make soldiers out of saints, had yet to be fought.

To please man with spectacular numbers and fascinating reports: or to please God with Africans conformed to the image of Christ – that was the choice that faced C. T. and his team. And they made it courageously.

It was a costly stand to take, but the standard raised at that time has endured as an undeviating principle in the main task of the mission, in planting truly sanctified and witnessing churches. However small in number, this must always be more pleasing to the Lord and more influential among the heathen, than a far larger body of mere professors of faith.

Despite the enormous discouragements, C. T. continued

to preach fearlessly that a new heart, filled with divine love for the Saviour and with divine hatred for sin, was essential to all who would live the Christian life. Without this new heart, he said, to seek to live a holy life, pleasing to God, was as ridiculous as to seek to cross a hundred yards above the Niagara Falls in a rowing boat!

"Don't be fooled," C. T. warned his fellow labourers. "Mice are not white asses because you hope them to be so. Sardines are not salmon because both wag their tails. Nor is a man a Christian just because he puts his hand up in a meeting and shouts hallelujah! Don't be taken in by the devil, nor by yourself, nor by men." C. T.'s conclusion was that a man or woman, black or white, *must* be filled with the Holy Spirit if he is to stand against all the wiles of the devil.

"We are not out here to please men or to make cheap reputations for ourselves," C. T. challenged each new arrival, "but to proclaim Christ's gospel of repentance and faith unto holiness. Our creed must be that 'without holiness no man shall see the Lord'."

1922 – Where are the reapers?

C. T. Studd moved south into a new area at the close of 1921, leaving a large band of workers to continue the teaching and establishing of churches in the northern area. Slowly the well-ordered village of Ibambi emerged out of the forest, with a palm-lined motor road running through its centre.

There was much to encourage, even in the midst of discouragements. Reinforcements were arriving in a steady flow, nine new workers reaching the field in 1921 and now sixteen in 1922! Jack Harrison, the future leader of the Congo work of the mission, and Jack Scholes, who would one day take over from Harrison, as well as Kerrigan, future Unevangelized Fields Mission (UFM) veteran, were among these.

The new intensive preaching of holiness did not diminish

the crowds who sat enthralled for hours listening to the Word. Never did Studd minister to such audiences as during the next ten years in the Ituri district. So challenging was his presentation of the gospel, powerful and searching and infinitely suited to the African mind by its simplicity of illustrations, that audiences would double in size when they knew that C. T. was to be the preacher. He would conduct evangelistic and holiness campaigns from Saturday to Thursday, folk coming from great distances with their food and bed-mat for "a real feast of good things!"

Norman Grubb, Alfred Ruscoe and Herbert Jenkinson were likewise building up the churches in the northern Welle area, visiting all the chieftains in turn. Their letters were thrilling, "having a glorious time . . . excellent service . . . never fitter and happier . . . a real inspiration . . . a glorious opening!" Herbert Jenkinson, future leader of the UFM, wrote: "What great lessons of self-sacrifice C. T. Studd has taught us since we came out here! I shall never be able to thank God enough for the privilege of working with him."

Leslie Sutton wrote in similar strain from Deti, on the eastern boundary of the work. The school was growing, and he was busy training a group of national evangelists to go out among the needy villages in the area. "All are a continual inspiration to me," he wrote.

However, amidst the joy, there was always that other note – the desperate need for more, and yet more, workers. Alfred Buxton ended one of his letters from Nala, with the words: "We ought to open four more stations at once, but we can't for our numbers are insufficient."

Ambrose, Holden and Staniford wrote from Wamba: "A great harvest is being lost while reapers delay!" They had trekked five days through the vast forest to the south-east, into as-yet unreached tribal areas, and had been well received. There was an urgent need to send a full-time worker there to teach the people and to consolidate the work, but who was available?

James Lowder, relieved of responsibility for Ibambi by

the arrival of C. T. Studd, trekked off further and further south, until he reached Bomili on the fast-flowing Aruimi River. A savage cannibalistic tribe, the centre of the terrifying leopard cult, the people nevertheless responded to the gospel, and "we had a glorious time!" wrote Lowder. "Four hours brought us to Chief Adangu's place, and practically the whole of his three villages turned to Christ!"

As he travelled on, he wrote: "Almost every village visited turned to God, and on leaving, the people implored us to remain. No missionary has yet been to Makara or Kandolole, and these many thousands have no one to shepherd them."

George Ambrose wrote of places "teeming with souls" around Ibambi. "Our great need now is reapers. If you could come to our Sunday meetings, you would discover that three-quarters of the congregation have walked for over an hour to get here, and many for two hours or more. During the last ten months, hundreds have been baptised. You can guess it is some work when you get about eight hundred souls seeking baptism and each one needs to be taught and tested individually." He was not grumbling, just longing for more workers, as was everyone else!

1923 – Taking a flying leap

"In the early days", Mrs Studd reminded the crowded congregation at the annual thanksgiving service, "C. T. said: 'Had I only seventy men, I could evangelise these four provinces in ten years!' Forty-six warriors have been sent out thus far, in the first ten years," she stated, and then challenged them all: "Can we send out twenty-four more during 1923 to make up the needed seventy?"

The verse that God gave the mission for that year was: "With Your help I can run through a barricade; with my God, I can scale a wall" (Ps. 18:29). "Let's make it a sprint and take a flying leap!" said Mrs C. T. And they did! Not only did twenty-four new workers sail for the Congo, but others also for Amazonia and Asia. This year was to see the beginning of the "worldwide" aspect of the vision coming into focus.

To the *Heart of Africa Mission*, parties sailed in May, July and December, including the first group of five workers from the United States of America and a further two from Norway, bringing the total work-force in the Congo up to seventy-one. Despite this, from all parts of the field, the reports kept coming in of the need for yet more workers.

But God was on the move, not only in the heart of Africa, but in bringing to birth the Heart of Amazonia Mission. "Full speed ahead!" were the marching orders to the first party of three men called to work among 300 Indian tribes of the Amazon Valley, as yet unreached with the gospel.

Bland, Knight and Hutcheson put their feet on Brazilian soil in June 1923, and set off to seek out the Carajas Indians on the Araguaya River, who, wrote the small intrepid group, "though lost in the jungles of ignorance and superstitions, are those whom Christ came to seek and to save!"

"The scientist has invaded these forests to study their peoples," one reported. "The traveller has passed from river to river in his search for new lands. Slave traders have invaded like a swarm of devastating locusts, the agents of wholesale massacres. Hard labour, violence and ill treatment have brought death to thousands of Indians, some tribes being obliterated for ever. But the messengers of the Cross have been content to stay at home to discuss the matter!"

Then came the birth of the Heart of Arabia Mission in the heart of Charles Miller, who with his wife and two children, was working in Cairo. His house lad, Zackie, through helping Miller in the translation of the Scriptures, came to know Christ as Saviour. Zackie got to know some Muslims who were willing to listen to the gospel, and brought them to Miller that they might hear "the good words of the Scriptures". One of these, Boutrous (Peter), a bedouin, soon yielded to Christ and openly confessed his faith in the market place, and then declared to Miller his desire "to go to Arabia to win his people to Christ". Then another, Awad Yohanna (John), openly declared *his* faith in Christ. As Miller and Boutrous passed by, they overheard Muslims saying: "There go the men that made Awad an unbeliever."

An extraordinary letter from Baghdad was the next step. The writer, Paul Attisha, was a Chaldean-Arab of Iraq, who had been won to God by a gracious American gentleman telling him of the One who hears and answers prayers, and directing his attention to the Scriptures. "I have sought and found Christ," Paul wrote, "whom my soul loves, and this love is leading me to action. I desire to obey the laws of His love in responding to His call to be His witness. Being an Arab citizen, and fully conversant with the language, habits, customs, mode of life and ways of the country, I hearken to the Lord's command in offering myself to God for the evangelisation of Arabia."

1924 – Among the Red Men

Fenton Hall, a man of magnificent physique, standing two metres tall in his socks, champion boxer, leading lawn tennis player of the British Army, powerful swimmer and diver, first-class football player, had nevertheless the great charm of absolute simplicity. He was one of God's gentlemen.

He was a typical Irishman, with a quick sense of humour and utter fearlessness. Having gained a scholarship to the Woolwich training centre, he was commissioned in the Royal Garrison Artillery as a seventeen year old. Invalided out of the Army, he was seconded to the Royal Air Force in 1921. Through the Officers' Christian Union, Fenton was led to a knowledge of Christ as his own personal Saviour, and never doing anything by halves, he immediately concentrated his whole being on living absolutely and only for his new Lord and Master, Jesus Christ.

On joining the Missionary Training Colony, Fenton threw himself into every aspect of training, preparing himself for any eventuality in his future service. It was during his time at the Colony that he received God's clear call to go to the Indians with the Heart of Amazonia branch of the WEC.

He sailed on May 23rd, 1924 from Liverpool to Maranham, near the mouth of the Amazon. Having spent two and a half months in the study of Portuguese, he set off in September by canoe for the Guajajara Indians, twenty villages about a week's journey up the Pindare River. His diary records: "What a glorious thing to be the first perhaps who shall carry to them the gospel which can lift them out of the pit and from the miry clay and set their feet on a Rock and establish their goings!"

Wherever they stopped to pass the night, he seized the opportunity to preach the gospel. At last he reached the home of a Christian Brazilian farmer and his family, where he stayed for a while, "only two days' journey from the nearest Guajajara village," and here he started work on learning their language.

On October 6th he went forward, barefooted and taking nothing with him, but what he could carry on his back, "to win the Indians for Christ."

For the next two months he laboured unceasingly amongst the dark-skinned "red men". By day, bare-backed, he worked with them in the forest, to prove to them that he came to them like his Master, to serve and not to be served. By night, he preached to those who would listen. He ate their food and slung his hammock on the verandahs of their huts.

"I spent all day felling trees", he recorded, "and made a very bad hand at it. It amuses them to have a mad white man with them, clad as they are in nothing but trousers and a belt, attempting to do the same work as they do, and eating their grub. At night we sing a hymn or two, and I preach the gospel, but I don't know how much they understand. God has given me a real love for these people and a real craving to win them for Christ."

He moved from village to village; one particular trek was to be the last. His bare feet still had not acclimatised to the rough paths, and he suffered much from septic sores. They had little food and often went to bed hungry. His diary commented that he was not feeling too well, and he found it hard to concentrate on Bible study and preparation for his evening preaching. But there was no complaint, other than with himself.

After describing a particularly difficult day, there was a break in Fenton's diary, as he suffered a severe attack of dysentery. He became weaker and wearier, until at one stopping place he completely collapsed, suffering intermittently from high fever. He was too weak to do anything more, and those with him put up his hammock and lifted him into it.

"I knew I was on the verge of death from exhaustion," he scribbled a few days later. "For three to four hours, I experienced the terrible power of the devil. My effort was to have absolute submission to and trust in God – leaving everything to Him, casting all my care upon Him. The devil fought me inch by inch. He used Scripture, science, reason, learning, knowledge and wisdom. How I wished that I knew nothing! He used my great weakness as a Christian. I got to doubt my own salvation. In the end, somehow, God won."

Up to December 5th he tried to continue to write his diary daily, speaking of indigestion troubles and the distress of his poor feet, but otherwise praising God. Three days later, there was a pencilled addition to the Home Overseer of the mission, with a small PS, "Yes, I *will* rejoice, *rejoice* in the Lord and in the God of my salvation."

Suddenly his letters stopped. Many weeks passed with no news. At last a cable came: "Hall died of fever December 25th at Sapucaia."

1925 – Can you not make Crusaders more quickly?

"Over twenty million heathen in six unevangelised regions is the immediate object of the Crusade," shouted the announcement of the twelfth Annual WEC Meeting, to be held in the Central Hall, Westminster.

In the four corners of the poster, one could read of:

"The Heart of Africa – and on into Chad and Sudan!"
"The Heart of Amazonia – and up river to the Amahuaca tribe!"
"The Heart of Arabia – and through to Asia and Afghanistan!"

and so to the final corner:

"The Heart of *anywhere* – without Christ!"

The challenge was clear. The call to push back the frontiers of heathendom and to take "the whole wide world for Jesus" was engraved, not only on the badges, but also in the hearts, of every Crusader!

During 1925, seventeen new missionaries were sent at the April Valedictory Rally, but rather than merely rejoicing at these reinforcements, cries came home from field after field: "Can you not make Crusaders more quickly? The fields are open for the reapers, but where are they? Please come quickly!"

Throughout the Congo field, in the Heart of Africa Mission, it was a year of consolidation. Through the work among the women and schoolchildren, through the clinics and technical schools, out in the villages and all along forest pathways, people were getting right with God and burning their witchcraft whistles, learning to read and preparing for baptism.

The Heart of Amazonia Mission's small team were hard at language study, practising in the homes of Portuguese businessmen who wanted to learn English. They drew a map of the whole Amazon basin, with its vast network of rivers, and tried to mark in all the larger tribes of Indians. A plan of campaign was drawn up, to attack the "enemy stronghold" from three angles.

So they had sailed from Portugal to the mouth of the Amazon, on to Carolina, and were now pressing westwards to the river Tapajos and the Chipaya Indians. The second advance ought to be one thousand miles up the Amazon River to Manaos, then by boat a further two thousand miles south-west up the river Jurua to Iquitos, and so by mail steamer southwards along the Ucayali River for yet another six hundred miles, to reach the Amahuaca Indians. Thirdly, "when more Crusaders became available", an advance should be made from Manaos, further westwards along the Caquara River, towards the foothills of the mighty Andes, to reach the Tukano Indians.

"Some of these Indians are cannibals," they wrote, "eating the heart and powdered bones of their dead relations. Many are sun-worshippers. All have suffered terribly at the hands of unscrupulous traders and there is a high death toll through the prevalence of beri-beri and other diseases. Yes, all that is true, but these are people for whom Christ died."

Despite every discouragement, the small team were pressing ahead, and kept pleading with the home-end to "send us more workers as fast as you can! The task is vast, time is running out on us, and we are so few!"

For the Heart of Asia Mission, H. E. Ward, the first WEC pioneer, was just about to leave for the border of Afghanistan, when a most stirring report was received from Rolla Hoffman, an American missionary, who had just entered that strange and little known land. "Our first visit to the city of Herat", he wrote, "marks another milestone in the advance of the forces of Christ in Central Asia."

Hoffman had gained entrance by offering medical help, as the Afghan government had strictly forbidden any religious activity. In the first nine days, his team of four missionaries had seen 748 patients in an improvised office, as well as countless others out in the yard and on the stairway. The overwhelming medical needs, though on a scale previously unimagined, paled into insignificance against the shattering spiritual needs of these as-yet un-reached peoples.

"The challenge of Afghanistan has always had its place in our thoughts and prayers and plans," wrote Hoffman. "But now we have beheld the need for ourselves. We have seen the eager sufferers crowding past the guards and pressing into the consulting room with outstretched hands to grasp our garments in entreaty. We have heard the cry of that needy people . . . calling, calling . . . until we can go again – to heal their bodies, yes, but also to win their hearts for our Lord."

The whole report rang in the ears of the WEC pioneer as a clear Macedonian call: "Come over and help us!"

1926 – Renewed marching orders

At the same time as the Lord was powerfully blessing, trouble continued to brew in the mission. The devil was not going to take the invasion of his territory lying down! How better to fight back than to attack the leadership, and the fellowship between the missionaries?

In the Congo, stories began to spread, bringing con-fusion and strange accusations. C. T. Studd was becoming increasingly weak and so unable to visit each member of his team, as he had always sought to do in the past. In pain from gallstones and hampered with frustrating asthma attacks, he nevertheless would not "give in and go home", as many advised him to do. Medical friends had provided him with pain-killing drugs, and he kept going with the help of these, taking "just sufficient to enable me to keep on my feet, and keep talking for Jesus!"

The first major rumour was that C. T. had become a drug addict. Assurances were given that the morphia supplied to him through a kindly doctor of the Africa Inland Mission in Nairobi was only used sparingly to alleviate pain, but doubts persisted in the minds of some.

Secondly, it was rumoured that C. T. was now preaching "another doctrine", substituting "salvation by works" for the pure gospel of "salvation by grace through faith". It was true that Studd was, and always had been, adamant that the Church of Jesus Christ must be a holy Church: that converts must show the fruit of the Holy Spirit in their lives. It was inconceivable to C. T. that one could be truly born again into the family of God and yet remain in deliberate sin: yet there was absolutely no shift in doctrinal belief.

A statement was clearly printed to this effect in the November magazine, yet eighteen out of the sixty-eight missionaries in the Congo resigned from the WEC at the close of 1925. Heart-broken, C. T. called his local missionary group together, and they spent a prolonged period of time in prayer and fasting, in searching the Scriptures and their hearts, to receive renewed "marching orders" from the King of kings. C. T. longed to see his untrained "company" turned into a disciplined "army".

They were reading in Hebrews chapter eleven, when the fire fell upon them. "As the Holy Spirit had filled those ancient saints with a lust for sacrifice for God and a joy which crucifies all human weakness," wrote C. T.'s biographer, "so He could fill these modern-day Crusaders." What was the condition? "Sell out!" Would they? "They would!"

It was a new company that left C. T.'s hut that night, with laughter on their faces, a sparkle in their eyes, and love unspeakable burning in their hearts, for each had become a "devotee-to-death for the glory of the Saviour." The joy of battle possessed them! WEC did not die, as some had predicted it would but came forth into more abundant life than ever before.

From that time on, throughout the mission, there was a new love, unity and joy, in sacrifice and zeal for souls. No one murmured if funds were short: no one wanted to go on furlough. Married couples put the needs of the young Church even before those of their own families. Single women "manned" many of the lonely outposts and never shirked to do their part, whatever the cost. Companions willingly agreed to separate in order to double their effectiveness. Even in bereavement, Crusaders triumphed and God was glorified.

Someone wrote home about C. T. at that time: "The sight of the old warrior is an inspiration and a rebuke. Without having had one day's holiday in ten years, he works from 4 a.m. to 10 p.m. and often does not relax even for meals but just eats at odd times the food brought to him at his desk. His small mud-floored room does for bedroom, dining-room and study. In the corner stands his old native bed with strips of animal hide instead of springs, covered with a few blankets and hard-looking pillows, on which four hours' sleep is considered a good night's rest. At odd moments, mostly at night, he has translated more than eight epistles, Psalms, Proverbs and a large number of hymns."

During that difficult year, five great centres of light broke out among the myriads of Wabudus and Balikas around Ibambi, tribesmen who were said to touch rock-bottom in fallen humanity.

Chief Adzangwe, one of the worst cannibals and ringleaders in all evil in the Ibambi area, was miraculously changed. He became a leader in his local church and fervent in evangelism. When imprisoned for his fiery zeal, he led prisoners to the Lord!

At Adzoka, the first missionary to arrive was beaten up and mobbed by a furious yelling crowd, all waving sticks, knives, bows and arrows. Then God broke through, and some hundred and twenty gathered daily to be taught in the Word before going to work. Over five hundred gathered on Sundays for worship, and the singing nearly raised the roof.

A stiff fight went on at Bakondongama's church, sandwiched between two bitterly hostile chiefs. Few came to hear the gospel: still fewer showed any sign of change.

No one brought food for the missionaries, nor cared for them when sick. Suddenly, all was different – the church full, the schools overflowing, food pouring in, and lives marvellously changed!

The revival that had broken out in Badua's territory shattered all complacency. Cannibalism, witchcraft and hemp-smoking suddenly gave way to changed lives and overwhelming joy. A new church was built to hold six hundred, rather than the sixty previously. The roof was tied on by string from the wine-palms of converted drunkards! The crowds squeezed in so tight there was barely room for the speaker – all this among a tribe with a reputation of being too dangerous for a white man to live among them!

1927 – God's cyclone!

In his reminiscences of his wife, after her death in 1929, C. T. recalled how he went home from the Congo in 1915 "to get recruits", and how he found his dear wife half bed-ridden with illness and weakness. "Surely," he wrote, "God was waiting for some simple act of faith to send down His blessing. That blessing hit my wife the very day after I left again for the Congo, and she was never the same woman again! She became a cyclone, the mission's chief deputation secretary as well as a great many other things beside.

"She had often wanted to come out here," C. T. reminisced in his small hut at Ibambi, "but that I would never allow, for I knew it was mere suicide on her part: she could never have stood the heat. Moreover, I knew she would be far more service to God and the mission and even to me, at home and elsewhere than out here."

How in the end did he permit her, then, to come out to Africa?

"When we were first married," he recalled, "we entered into a contract with God that we would neither of us ever keep the other back from doing any work that God laid before us. God was wonderfully gracious. All our earlier years He had kept us together – in China ten years, in India seven years, and in between times in England. Then came the founding of this mission; but when that took place neither of us dreamed that it would involve a very long separation" – eleven long years of patient sacrifice, in fact.

Then the marvellous reunion took place.

"In 1927, my wife was travelling through the Mediterranean and landed in Egypt," C. T. recorded. "The opening of motor roads made it possible for her to reach us in two days after leaving Rejaf on the Nile, so I wired an invitation for her to come, not only from myself but from all the missionaries in Congo.

"I knew perfectly well that she wanted me to come home, but that would never do," C. T. continued, almost dispassionately. "I also knew that her permanently staying in the heart of Africa, was an impossibility: she would have speedily gone to heaven! So I said, 'Come, and we will all pray together, and consecrate our lives afresh as of old. In all our young days God kept us together. Now it is a small thing that He should ask in our old age that we should yield each other up to Him to execute this work of evangelisation. We will meet once again, and then we will part for ever till we meet in heaven, you to do the work in England that I am convinced that nobody else but you can do, and me to do the work here that is equally demanded of me.'"

So she came, and Priscilla Studd, lovingly known to all as Mrs C. T., had the opportunity to visit the work in the Congo, and for two short weeks to be reunited with her beloved husband in the place dearest to both their hearts.

All marvelled at the way God used her to speak to the hearts of the Africans. Few ever forgot her words. "It was a joy to be on the same platform as her," wrote C. T., "though her presence was an agony to me, as I could see the terrible cost to her every day that she spent here. She pleaded with me to be allowed to stay, and almost became rebellious! Then how she prayed that I would go home with her. But there was never any doubt in our minds when the real word of command came from God."

And so it was that they parted, never to meet again down here on earth.

When Mrs C. T. arrived home on June 3rd, and gave her report of the whole Congo work, she had to answer the urgent question: "How did you find C. T.?" excruciatingly painful though the telling of it proved to be.

"After eleven years," she said, "there were bound to be changes, but I was not prepared for so great a change in him. I found the shell of C. T., a frail form, the shadow of C. T. I found a body spent and bent from long hours sitting in one position, bending over a table, translating . . . I found a spectre, the ghost of my former husband . . . He moved and talked as one of another world. I found such a man as Paul describes, 'I keep under my body and bring it into subjection,' a man with his face marred and body buffeted. YET behind all this frailty and brokenness, this poor shrivelled-up body, I found a giant mentally and spiritually. Thus I found C. T.!"

1928 – Dawn in the Devil's Den

There are so many unsung heroes of those pioneer days: how can one select a few to represent all the others? In the Heart of Africa Mission, there was Herbert Jenkinson, future leader of the Unevangelised Fields Mission. As a twelve year old, he had responded to an appeal at the close of a Boys' Brigade company meeting, of which he then became a keen and enthusiastic member. Stories told of Carey, Morrison, Mackay and Livingstone thrilled this young lad's heart. Testimonies of converts such as Pastor Tshi, Samuel Crowther, Chief Khama and many others, quickly drew him to see the value of missionary work.

Then, "one day in 1915," Herbert recalls, "the captain of our Brigade Company told me that a famous missionary was to visit our church, and that I must be sure to be there.

As I arrived at our church hall, a taxi pulled up at the side gate, which I knew was locked, so I went to point out the correct entrance. Out stepped a tall distinguished gentleman with a fine Van Dyke beard and an overcoat almost down to his ankles. I delivered my message, but instead of going round to the entrance, the visitor vaulted over the wall! That was my first encounter with C. T."

C. T. had spoken on "Dawn in the Devil's Den" and from that evening onwards Herbert knew that God had called him to the Congo. He devoured every bit of WEC literature that came his way, even reading the mission's magazine in the trenches during World War One. At last came the day of sailing for the "Devil's Den".

"To this day," testifies Herbert, "I can well remember my first trek to the forest villages and the joy of preaching the gospel to people so willing to listen. What a lot has happened in the intervening sixty years," he goes on. "The gospel has been preached over a large area of Congo/Zaïre. Thousands have come to know the Lord Jesus Christ as Saviour, and His Church has been firmly established in what had been 'The Devil's Den'."

In the Heart of Amazonia Mission, two Australian Crusaders, Pat Symes and Fred Roberts, were tirelessly trekking amongst the Indian tribesmen of Sapucaia. They may not have been very successful at catching fish in the local rivers, but God mightily blessed their efforts amongst Indians, half-castes and Portuguese. House building, hunting for food, learning the language were all means to preach the gospel, and slowly, one by one, they had the joy of leading young folk to trust in the Lord.

Difficulties abounded. Superstitions ruled the lives of the Indians, so when sickness hit the small band of new believers and some died, their stand for Christ was blamed. The political authorities were threatening the missionaries, because of lying witness given by terrified tribesmen. Pat and Fred were plagued with several recurring bouts of fever. Dark clouds seemed to lie heavily over the whole area, as Christ's messengers challenged the devil's right to rule.

Yet, the men wrote of "bright rays of sunshine breaking through the clouds". As the two pressed on, trekking
by river and forest trail, they began to record the "readiness
with which many listen to the gospel," some giving
evidence of true conversion to God.

The Heart of Asia Mission's Jock Purves had joined Rex
Bavington, to work alongside the Central Asia Mission.
Urdu and Ladakhi languages had to be tackled. Rowing
skiffs up river and trudging through mountain passes
became daily occurrences. On one trek, the blanket-
clothed ponymen all declared it was impossible to cross
the Deosai Pass when thick snow and low lying clouds
descended on them. "We and the ponies will all die,"
they moaned.

But had not God said: "With Me all things are possible"?

So they struck camp and set off. They climbed over
rugged paths and up boulder-strewn streams, along narrow
ledges overlooking precipitous cliffs, across barren mountain sides, wading through ice-cold rivers, always looking
up to the snows, until at last, 15,600 feet up, they looked
down into Baltistan, "a land without Jesus Christ: a land
whose people have not yet had the Bible written for them: a
land largely unknown and unexplored."

Jock wrote of Baltistan as an unevangelised land of
70,000 Mongolian Buddhists, with but the two of them
amongst them, and he pleaded for reinforcements to join
them. "When *this* land is occupied," he added, "will you
allow me to go to Afghanistan where there are tens of
millions of square miles, holding millions of souls – and no
evangelists? Afghanistan: none. Tibet: none. Russian Turkestan: none. Central Mongolia: none. Nepal and Bhutan:
none. Here in Little Tibet, we solitary two. Oh, it is
shameful! Oh, Lord God, for Jesus' sake send forth the
labourers into the harvest! Millions of souls – and no
reapers – not even sowers yet!" And again he cried: "Do
please pray and consider my going to Afghanistan. I am
considering learning Pushtu now, though this will be three
languages on the go! Remember me, that Jesus will get

every ounce of me for the glory of His Name in the evangelisation of the world."

1929 – "She was not, for God took her"

Alfred Buxton had had to leave the field for health reasons in 1924. Now at last he was able to make a short visit. "January 30th, 1929 was a red-letter day if ever there was one," he wrote. "We met again!" What overwhelming joy that reunion with C. T. brought them both, as if there had been no intervening time.

Yes, C. T. was older and weaker and without some of his former vigour, Alfred recorded, but . . . phew! Preaching in and around Ibambi, writing innumerable letters, translating Scriptures, composing hymns – the old warrior was never still: the fire still burned. Maybe some folk didn't always appreciate the language in which he couched his letters and pamphlets – "Pungent language," Dan Crawford called it, "but his blunt reality revolted from all the studied straining after effect in the production of the expected stiff mode of clerical phraseology. When you listen to C. T. there is no fear of being lost in the labyrinths of language and logic. He gives it the gospel, hot and strong, and you must take him on his own terms for he lives the life. Here is a man supremely himself, racy yet real, with an undercurrent of tragic intensity. The semi-slang of his off-hand narrative is surely all the more sacred when it covers the bleeding heart of a husband and father torn from wife and family."

When the home-end asked C. T. to consider "Sabbath rest and periodic breaks for his health's sake," C. T. wrote: "I would be delighted to do so if we could only get an agreement from his majesty down in the regions below to take the same break. I regret to say he has refused. So I would ask you to pray for me, that I may continue to go at a break-neck gallop into heaven. I am getting, in my old age, to have a great respect for the devil, for at least he has this virtue, he is always at it and never tires of his job. My! What Christians we would be, what a sight for angels and men, if we would only fight for Christ as the devil fights against Him."

"It beats me how he endures," wrote Jim Grainger at the start of the same year. "Despite being ill earlier on, and still very weak and easily exhausted, he is hard at it all day. He spends himself for the Lord and these souls."

A week later came news that Mother Studd "was not, for God took her," while having a short rest in Spain.

Everyone who wrote of her in the following weeks spoke of her all-absorbing devotion to Christ. "No one would ever have accused her of lack of zeal for Christ if she had settled down to a life of ease as an invalid," wrote the General Secretary of WEC. "Instead of this, every hour of the day, and many hours of the night, were given to arduous work and to earnest wrestling with God. She was forever fighting with the greatest determination against physical weakness, and her sheer pluck, plus the blessing of God, lifted her above all inabilities of the flesh, and enabled her to do exploits."

All spoke of her prayer life. "There was something about Mrs Studd", Len Harris commented, "that no one could describe. She radiated the atmosphere of heaven, and how often her prayers brought me personally into the very presence of God. No book will be able to explain this. One only met it when one met her."

When the news reached the Congo, C. T. bowed his head, and then calmly and bravely declared: "This means we must be *hotter than ever*!" He had always spoken of death as a friend, not a foe; as promotion, not pain; emphasising that the joy of Christ's presence for the loved one far outweighed the sorrow of the human separation.

"Of course I knew her as no one else knew her," he wrote to the home staff. "I have always regarded her as a very wonderful woman. There were things about her that I have never met in any other woman, and in fact, I would sooner have had her to speak with me on any platform than almost any man that I know. God had given her a way of laying hold of an audience that very, very few have ever received, in my opinion. She made you see the things she spoke of, while she was speaking."

"Well," he went on, "God has taken her to Himself. We could well have done with her for many more years. And yet there is a sort of triumph with me in her being removed upstairs to do an even greater work than what she could do down here. The triumph of all this is that God is testing our faith, and our faith is going to come out as gold, for never for one moment will we believe anything else but that through the mighty power of Jesus her absence from the earth shall mean a greater blessing to us and the mission, than if she was abiding with us still. We know God has made no mistake, and we tell Him so. We shall praise Him as we've never praised Him before, because He has taken our beloved and is saying to us: 'Said I not unto thee that if thou would'st believe thou should'st see the glory of God?' Yes, indeed we and the mission will be yet greater super-conquerors than we ever could have been had she not been removed from amongst us. So let us praise God for His grace in taking her to be a fellow-worker with Him up there," he concluded, "and praise God that He has counted us faithful, and that we should not shrink back, but shall recognise that the greater the cross, so the greater the power and the glory that He will be able to pour upon His work down here."

1930 – "Now then – do it!"

"Christianity is based on *sacrifice*." So wrote young Jack Harrison, the truth having been burned into his heart through eight years of working closely alongside his fiery leader, C. T. Studd.

This was the keynote of a six-day conference held by the

Heart of Africa Mission, when 3,000 Africans came together to learn more of the things of God and to renew their vows of consecration to Him. Many of them had only recently been won from the horrors of cannibalism and witchcraft, but already they were learning the joy that comes to those who are "all out" for Christ.

There was the boy Mukwali, who had written to a lady missionary to say he had been reading the story of the ass that carried Jesus to Jerusalem, and that he had decided to be "an ass for Jesus" to carry Him to those around who had not yet learned of Him.

There was Lebo who had learned the joy of suffering for Christ. He had been beaten by his chief with twelve strokes of a hippo-hide whip, and between each lash had jumped up shouting: "Hallelujah! It's for Jesus!"

Grey-haired old Bakon was not there, for he was in exile because his jealous chief did not like to see the hundreds of people going to his village to learn of God.

"And are such as these to shame us Westerners, who think we are more enlightened?" questioned Jack. "Are these to press on and we missionaries lag behind? Is our love to be less warm than theirs? Our zeal less consuming? God forbid!"

"And what of the countless millions who have not yet heard of Him who died for them? The call is to all – not to a pious picnic but to a warfare! 'It is given to you on the behalf of Christ, not only to believe but also to suffer for His sake.' This demands a hazarding of ALL for the sake of souls without Christ."

"Then," challenged Jack, "if you covet to be numbered with those who loved not their lives unto death, but who overcame by the blood of the Lamb and the word of their testimony, present your bodies . . . this is your reasonable service! Anything short of this is unreasonable!"

"Now then – do it!" roared C. T. as an echo of General Booth's battle cry to his troops.

For seventeen years, C. T. had been "batting" away for God with the Heart of Africa Mission. Now many were fearful that if he did not take a break, he would not last much longer. As he would not heed warnings from the home-end, Alfred Buxton was asked to use his good offices to try and persuade the redoubtable batsman at least to accept a "lunch-interval". Alfred's visit to the Congo was ending and he would soon be travelling to East Africa and could take C. T. with him.

As he and Alfred travelled along the same route that they had taken in 1913, what memories must have stirred! Then there had been just the two of them: now there were over fifty.

In East Africa, during his short enforced holiday, C. T. addressed all sorts of groups, including CMS (Church Missionary Society) missionaries, the rising generation of African pastors and teachers, the white settlers' community and their children. He spoke of the dynamic power of Jesus, the Son of God, "to change cannibals into saints", and challenged all to take their part and "play the man!"

"C. T. certainly must realise", Alfred recorded, as the day of their parting approached (C. T. to return to the Congo, and Alfred to head northwards to Ethiopia), "that though sometimes heads may disagree with him, the hearts of God's people rejoice in his utter devotion to his Lord, and love and admire him for it, and not a few are seeking to follow." Keeping up the cricketing metaphor that so well fitted Studd's whole life, Alfred added, "May he complete his innings with many more boundary hits, and even carry his bat till stumps are drawn when the Lord comes!"

"You will be very glad to know", wrote Mrs Harrison to the home-end committee, shortly after C. T. had returned to Ibambi, "that C. T. is really very much better. He is away with my husband, for the opening of a new church at Mangbetu where the chief (who has four hundred wives) has said he will burn his witchcraft"!

"Our position is this for ever," wrote C. T. shortly afterwards. "We are out here to fight for Christ and see these people saved. Please tell everybody that whether we live or die in Christ's service here is a matter to us of no account whatever; only I believe we will be more happy to die for Christ than to live for Him. *We cannot be defeated.* Death is a real gain to us, it is our very own ambition!"

1931 – "Innings closed – run out"

"I saw with great regret," wrote Llewellyn Gwynne, Bishop of Egypt and Khartoum, "and yet with great pride, the account of the passing of dear old C. T. I look upon Studd as one of the most single-eyed, daring, self-sacrificing missionaries of the Cross ever sent by God to Africa. There was a good deal of the unalloyed, unsophisticated, early Christian about him, and his method of approach to the native of Africa must have been something like the methods employed by the first evangelists amongst the pagans of Asia Minor."

Just one of the many testimonies that streamed in after the cable to London in 1931: "Bwana glorified July 16."

"I want you to understand absolutely that this mission from its inception has been a worldwide mission and by no means one limited to Africa alone." Thus was C. T. busy reiterating the standards and principles of both doctrine and practice to his faithful band of fellow-labourers. "I believe that several times God has called a society to evangelise the world, and each could have done so, but each turned aside from the real path of God to please men. Now it is our turn. God has called us and tried us, and now He has brought us to the supreme test as to whether we will trust in *Him* alone or whether we will cringe or fear or pander to the Christian world. I believe if we stick steadfastly to God, that 'when He has tried us, we shall come forth as gold,' and therefore I am not the least afraid however few we become, so long as those few have their hearts set on God and God only. We need a great humility, a great courage, and, hallelujah, a great cheek too, but all these we can get from God. It is devil-may-care-ism we need! Forward!"

The voice grew fainter. He ceased to try to talk and with each little breath he could only say: Hallelujah! The old warrior's long fight was ended, in his seventy-first year, eighteen years after the doctors had warned him that it would be suicide to go to the heart of Africa. He had indeed finished the course and kept the faith.

Two thousand Africans managed to arrive at Ibambi in time for the funeral, and what a mighty time of rejoicing ensued! "The station was filled to overflowing," Ezeno reported. "At the graveside we made our vow, saying: 'Our father has thrown away his life for us; we want to throw away our lives in the fight of Jesus!'" Boimi, who was to become the director of the church of Jesus Christ in north-eastern Zaïre in the years ahead; Ndugu, a future leading pastor of the Ibambi church; Batu, the head boy of the local school; Isatu, C. T.'s fifteen year old personal "boy"; each in turn gave most moving testimonies, and, with thousands of others that day, renewed their consecration to God, to be "hotter than ever for Jesus!"

"His life stands as some rugged Gibraltar," Alfred Buxton wrote movingly of C. T., whom he always looked upon as his father, "a sign to all succeeding generations that it is worthwhile to lose all this world can offer and stake everything on the world to come. His life will be an eternal rebuke to easy-going Christianity. He has demonstrated what it means to follow Christ without counting the cost and without looking back."

"C. T. was essentially a cavalry-leader," he continued, "and in that capacity he led several splendid charges. He impersonated the heroic spirit, the apostolic abandon, which is so easy to lose from the work of Christ. His shortcomings were in reality the exaggeration of his unique qualities – his courage in any emergency, his determination never to sound the retreat, his conviction that he was in the will of God, his faith that God would see him through, his contempt of the arm of flesh, and his willingness to risk all for Christ.''

"It is written of Cranmer," Alfred went on, "that he worked all his life with the knowledge that the stake awaited him. In the same way, for twenty years, C. T. has had the sentence of death upon him, but he has gone steadfastly on to finish the work that he was given to do."

"His life was one great sacrifice," testified one. "God never fails to acknowledge and reward heroic faith. I know of no man whose faith 'stuck' so fiercely as C. T.'s, in season and out of season."

It was Mr F. de Courcy Hamilton who wrote: "He took good care to get no personal honour and even went out under a cloud. Few know how he coveted a life of extinction. Newspaper biographers acclaim him mostly for his performances in school and college days with the cricket bat – but he will have a wonderful time now that his *real innings has closed 'run out!'* His entrance to the Pavilion will be splendid, but I am sure he will cover his face and give all the credit of his marvellous harvest to the One who hired him, by laying down His life."

Part Two

FAITH

1932–1952

"And so we started again – in 1931," wrote Norman Grubb in his autobiography, *Once Caught, No Escape*. "There were only four of us at the home-end, and there came the question: 'What are you aiming for?' C. T. had gone, and the mission was in such ill-repute that there had only been fifty pounds that month for the thirty-five workers on the field, so hadn't we better close down? But the next thought was, 'What commission did your founder have, which he's passed on to you?' We knew that answer – to evangelise the world. 'Well, are you going to do it?' 'How can we in our present condition and this being the time of world financial depression?' Once again came the thought: 'How did the men of the Bible do the impossible?' and of course we knew the answer: 'By faith!'"

"What does faith mean in a practical sense?" Norman further queried. "We were led to look at Joshua, supposedly because he was in the same tight corner, having just lost his Moses. We saw that God talked with him and told him to go right forward, and to be strong and courageous. But then, when that interview finished, we read – and this is what caught us – that Joshua called together his officers and told them to prepare food, for in three days they would cross the Jordan. But who gave him authority to say that? Then we saw that when we are at God's general disposal to do His will, He puts Himself at our disposal to fill in the details. So it was Joshua who fixed on the three days' limit and God came through with the opening of the Jordan at the time fixed by Joshua."

"So we got started!"

"Give me the faith which can remove"

Give me the faith which can remove
　　And sink the mountains to a plain;
Give me the child-like praying love,
　　Which longs to build Thy house again;
Thy love, let it my heart o'erpower
And all my simple soul devour.

I would the precious time redeem,
　　And longer live for this alone,
To spend, and to be spent, for them
　　Who have not yet my Saviour known;
Fully on these my mission prove,
And only breathe, to breathe Thy love.

My talents, gifts and graces, Lord,
　　Into Thy blessed hands receive;
And let me live to preach Thy Word,
　　And let me to Thy glory live;
My every sacred moment spend
In publishing the sinners' Friend.

Enlarge, inflame, and fill my heart
　　With boundless charity divine:
So shall I all my strength exert,
　　And love them with a zeal like Thine;
And lead them to Thy open side,
The sheep for whom their Shepherd died.

Charles Wesley

1932 – And can it be?

"We have a multi-millionaire to back us up, out and away the wealthiest Person in the world," C. T. had written to a friend shortly before he died. "I had an interview with Him. He gave me a cheque book free, and urged me to draw upon Him. He assured me His firm clothed the grass of the field, preserved the sparrows, counted the hairs of His children's heads, knew what they needed before they asked, and even took thought for oxen who tread out the corn.

"He said the Head of the Firm promised to supply all our need, and to make sure, Two of the Partners were to go along with each member of our parties, and would never leave us or fail us. He even showed me some testimonials from former clients. One from an army man called Joshua, was very interesting. It began, 'Not one good thing hath failed.' Another said he had been pulled out of a horrible pit. A tough old chap, with a long beard and hard-bitten face, said on one occasion supplies had arrived and been delivered by black ravens, and at another, by a white-winged angel.

"And another little old man, who seemed scarred and marked all over like a walnut shell, said he had been saved from death times untold, for he had determined to put to the proof the assurance that he who would lose his life for the Firm's sake, should find it. He told stories more wonderful than the *Arabian Nights*, of escapes and hardships, travels and dungeons, and with such a fire in his eyes and laugh in his voice, added 'But out of them all, the Partner delivered me.'"

"It did me good to see this old warrior," C. T. had remarked. "He was like a bit of red-hot quick-silver, and one felt scorched up with shame in his presence."

What could possibly be an adequate memorial for such a giant?

Norman Grubb and his wife Pauline and their two faithful helpers at the mission's London headquarters looked around and said: "It *must* be more workers! If we are to begin to evangelise the world, we had better begin by immediate reinforcements to the Congo. As we prayed, God led us to claim twenty-five new workers – ten by the first anniversary of C. T.'s glorification, and another fifteen by the second." God alone was to be trusted both to call them and to send the money specifically for their out-going. They put their fingers on Mark 11:24, "Whatever you ask for in prayer, believe that you have received it, and it will be yours;" and took the first ten by faith.

"Another test came to me the next day," Norman relates. "It occurred to me that our Congo folks would not have buildings for ten extra ones, and I had better warn them. But wait a minute; supposing the 'ten' didn't come? I should look a fool, and the mission would look for another secretary, the same as if Joshua had failed to get that river opened. Of course, the source of that remark was obvious, and I settled it by going myself to the mailbox and putting in the letter."

Throughout the year, letters came constantly from all the fields, stressing the increasing needs. Mary Rees wrote of many turning to God. "The chief of the lepers said he will build a church . . . but we *need more workers*!"

Annie Mitchell told of two youths coming to the door and telling her of a village where "there is no one to teach us of Jesus. Could not someone come to our village?" "Such appeals go to the very depths of our souls," Annie wrote; "*Oh, send us workers!*"

"We only wish we had half a dozen pairs of hands and legs," wrote Mary Harrison, wife of the newly elected leader in the Congo, as she told of so many calls hither and thither of groups longing to be taught.

Then came the realisation that not only white missionaries were involved in the challenge for a worthy memorial to the Founder – but that God was saying there should be ten *black* workers also sent out "to push the battle to the gates".

The story of lame Zamu, who, with his wife, set off and trekked eighty miles south to the Bomili area, and then another ten days to reach the Balumbi tribe, thrilled everyone. "I have never met a tribe who are so asking for teachers as these people," Zamu reported. "When I teach them, they watch me so intently, that I thought they might be planning to eat me! No, they said: we are just wondering why such a young man as you should come from such a far away place to teach us!"

Then the great red-letter day – December 18th, 1931 – when eight more African missionaries, two men and their wives from Wamba and the same from Ibambi, set off with Sam Staniford for the south. "It is a big thing for these people", our missionaries wrote, "to go amongst tribes of quite a different language and culture."

The closing few days of the year before the anniversary of C. T.'s death were filled with miracles, so that all twenty, white and black, had been called, tried, accepted, equipped and sent on their way rejoicing. The tenth white missionary, Ivor Davis, was ready just ten days before the deadline date, and he was given, as his African name, Mr Ten. The last £200 for the finances came two days from the end.

"The thrill of this," recorded Norman, "was not so much the completion of the twenty as the confirmation that we were on the main line of the Bible principle of faith."

1933 – Dare we?

FAITH was now on the stretch. Could they believe for the further fifteen new missionaries whom they had already claimed for the next year?

It was a time of universal financial collapse. The mission itself was in almost desperate circumstances. During the first five months, not one new missionary was ready to go out. Then, suddenly, things began to move quickly, and three men sailed for the Congo.

The mission then received applications for no less than four other unevangelised lands – Colombia, Arabia, Little Tibet and Spanish Guinea – and they realised that, "The Fifteen" were to be scattered in different fields to begin to carry out C. T.'s worldwide vision of occupying every unoccupied region with the gospel.

Pat Symes and Nesta Keri Evans sailed for Colombia: Gwyneth Rees and Keith Stevenson were ready for Arabia: Alec and Mrs Dora Thorne were called by God for Spanish Guinea: Rex and Mrs Bavington and Daniel Voumard were poised for Little Tibet: Ivy Milliken came in, called to the Congo: and only a few days before the deadline, the last two of the fifteen, Harold Wood and John Harbison, offered for Colombia!

God had completed "The Fifteen", with all the money needed for their equipment and passages, AND enabled the entrance into Spanish Guinea, Little Tibet and Colombia, all in that one year.

Let some of the new missionaries tell their own stories. *To Spanish Guinea*: Australians Alec Thorne and his wife Dora had been independent missionaries in Morocco when God called them, at forty-four years of age, to join WEC and to "invade" Spanish Guinea for Him. On arrival, two German traders had made them welcome, and provided them with temporary accommodation and food.

"Today has been a day of facing out a few vital facts with God alone," Alec wrote one week later. "I have *not* got the necessary qualifications for a pioneer. Am I an absolute fool to come out here like this? Is it to be a case of showing up the utter folly of WEC methods? Well, God called me to leave Morocco and come here, so I must also believe that He can do what He will without regard to the human quality of the materials available!"

After three months of intensive language study, they plunged into the interior on their first trek to the Okak tribe.

"Off on the trail at last. Roads very bad, streams in plenty. Rocks galore and hills too many to count. Eighteen miles first day, enough for a greenhorn at trekking. Tried for the first time to speak twenty words of a message and to pray in the language. I believe they actually understood!"

By the end of that first month's trek, God had led them to the village where they were to settle, given them a temporary home, acceptance with the local people and, perhaps the most wonderful gift of all, an ability with the language. *To Central Asia*: "Does the life of faith work?" That had been the big question in Rex Bavington's heart when he came home on furlough in 1928, after his first three arduous years in Baltistan. "At first, it had all been so exciting," he testified. "Jock and I lived in a little native shack with mud floors, crawling with vermin, rats, fleas, lice and bugs. We were never clean, and life was literally 'the laugh of faith!'"

"In those early days," Rex recollects, "there was spiritual power because we were flat out in the race in stark naked faith, believing God; and souls were snatched out of the twilight of Islam. But I have to confess," he continues, "that like a fool, I forsook, slowly but surely, the way of God's millionaires and entered the rank and file of paupers." Then he tells how for five years he chose a softer job and left the life of faith.

"What a terrible experience God's second best is," he cried out at last. Remembering that "God called Jonah a second time", Rex and his wife, with one year old twins, rejoined WEC in 1933 for work in Central Asia, once again with Jock Purves. They had recaptured the vision, that forsaking all else, they were to trust God alone and be flat out for Him.

To Colombia: In somewhat similar ways, God was also dealing with Pat Symes. Discontented, on furlough from his first term in Brazil, he resigned from WEC. But then God began to lay on his heart the need of the Republic of Colombia. WEC were praying about opening a work there, and asking God to send an experienced missionary to them to launch out. God brought the two needs together, and Pat rejoined WEC in 1933 and sailed for Buenaventura, in order to establish a mission work in the heart of the Andes. Crossing mountain range after mountain range, passing through fantastic countryside 12,000 feet high, with a glorious view of the plain below, Pat had reached his target, and cabled home: "August 10th, 1934. Bogota, Colombia: a city with a population of 235,000, clean and with every modern convenience, but very needy as far as the gospel goes."

Little did Pat then guess of the horrors and cruelty that lay ahead, before those needy people would open their hearts and accept the gospel that he had come to proclaim. But one thing he did know for sure, it was God who had sent him there, and he was not going to be disobedient to the heavenly vision.

1934 – God enabling us, we go on

Readers who have followed the Story of the Ten and the Story of the Fifteen will have already noted that we are asking the Lord for no less than twenty-five new missionaries before July 16th, 1934, the third anniversary of Mr Studd's death. To some it may seem ridiculous or even presumptuous to ask such an increase in these days of depression – but to others twenty-five seems all too small in the face of the millions still without a ray of light.

So read the introductory paragraph in the mission's January magazine.

The Congo were preparing to commemorate this same third anniversary of the death of WEC's founder in a different way – with a conference, "to be the greatest national conference ever held by the Heart of Africa Mission." Chiefs and their people, from tribes who had never before sent representatives, were expected to attend from a radius of 200 miles. An outdoor meeting place "of a thousand poles" was being erected.

Traders, government officials and cotton agents were all watching, anticipating unmitigated disaster as so many tribes came together – could God prove that "All one in Christ Jesus" was just as real for black Keswicks as white?

During the year Pat Symes, claiming five of the new twenty-five, continued to write of the *fight*: "Holiness comes into every sermon, for it is the thing that hits them hardest. As far as I can see, it is the one proof of Christianity." And the devil didn't like it! He fought back ferociously against the small courageous band.

Alec Thorne told how they were "up against it in Spanish Guinea". Amidst all the problems of poor housing, little food, ill health, government opposition, yet they could write: "Oh, yes, the Lord will bring us through, but it is evidently *through*, not round, the opposition! Problems yes, galore – but the one thing we came out to see is also here, hunger and response among the natives. Oh, do make people understand that whole towns are asking, asking, *asking* for someone to come and teach them!"

From Little Tibet, news trickled through that Rex Bavington had been asked to join the International Himalayan Expedition – truly a novel way for doing missionary work, even in the ranks of the WEC! He was needed because of his knowledge of the Hindustani language. "My main job is with the crowd of 600 load carriers, honest Little Tibetans, men from dozens of tucked-away villages all round the valley, whom no witness of the message of salvation has ever been able to reach. I am having grand opportunities of witnessing," Rex continued. "I have never seen so many Baltis together at one time in one place before, so I am doing an aggressive evangelistic tour!"

Then broke the news of the "10,000 shouting Hallelujah!" at the greatest conference ever held in the Congo. One visitor wrote: "I have never seen a more on-fire group of missionaries! They live for souls and are ready to die for them. Prayer is being made night and day, round the clock – no wonder miracles are happening. The spirit of sacrifice of their glorified leader is here indeed!"

Alfred Ruscoe had gone out from Canada to take part in this amazing conference and wrote: "What a sea of faces, and how they sang! I could hardly restrain myself from tears. The unity among the people, black and white, is fantastic. I have never seen the like before."

"Oh, praise the Lord!" wrote a veteran missionary. "Nine tribes, who a few years ago were at each other's throats, are now enjoying each other's fellowship in the Lord, inviting each other to eat from the same food dish – impossible some years back."

Just then came the news that the twenty-five new missionaries had been accepted and commissioned – fourteen men and eleven women – for the Congo, Colombia, Ivory Coast, Little Tibet and Portuguese Guinea. Praise God for His wonderful faithfulness! Dare they now claim *seventy-five* more, spread over the next three years? The needs were there and the labourers were few: so the conditions were right for obedience to God's command: "Ask the Lord of the Harvest to send out workers into His harvest field."

1935 – Operation Tooth Coast!

"West Africa needs you, Sta!"

On furlough after a long spell of service in the Congo, Sam and Lilian Staniford could hardly believe their spiritual ears. They had promised the Congolese a speedy return, once Sam's double cataracts had been successfully dealt with. They were now ready, poised to go back to the land they loved.

"Ivory Coast, in West Africa, needs you." The voice of God was persistent.

News had filtered through of the many small coastal tribes, between Liberia and Ghana, who had been resisting the nefarious traffic in "black ivory". Slave traders and exploiters; colonisers and civilisers; but no evangelists of the gospel were working among the sin-enslaved tribes of Ivory Coast. Spiritual darkness brooded over the one and three-quarter million people in this vast area.

The message of "Prophet Harris", the Liberian evangelist, who had trekked through the region more than ten years before, had evoked a remarkable response. Hundreds of fetishes had been burnt and whole villages had turned from their evil ways to seek the living God. But the government of the day, fearful of the influence of this English-speaking "foreigner", had banned him, and many of the hundred thousand converts had drifted back into heathenism.

Then Fred Chapman had "turned up, somewhere in the British Midlands," to quote his own testimony. Brought up in a godly home, one of seven children, Fred had early given his heart to the Lord Jesus, and knew at once that God wanted him for the mission field, but it was not until he was in his late twenties that he moved forward into training for missionary service.

He went to Cliff College, and there at a missionary prayer-meeting he was challenged to the depths of his being by one of the visiting speakers, Norman Grubb, General Secretary of WEC! "The Lord spoke so clearly to me: 'Join yourself to this group – for the sake of souls in Ivory Coast': so I gave in my name at the close of the meeting, to receive further information regarding WEC."

Reading the life story of C. T. Studd during the following term finally clinched Fred's call – except for one problem. He knew his call was to Ivory Coast, and Norman Grubb insisted that WEC had no work in Ivory Coast!

As he travelled down to the London headquarters of WEC to start his candidate's training, Fred asked God to give him three "seals", that he might be absolutely certain that it was God who was sending him, and no will-o'-the-wisp fancy of his own. Firstly, he asked God for a companion, preferably a man, experienced in missionary service and who knew and loved Africans: secondly, the money needed for fare and equipment: and thirdly, that Norman Grubb and the committee would remember, without any need for him to remind them, that he had said that Ivory Coast was to be the place of his appointment!

"Truly, God had gone before me," he recalls with relish. "As I opened the gates, I was greeted excitedly by a fellow student: 'Have you heard the news about Sam Staniford? He has been called by God to go with you to Ivory Coast!' Then he added: 'Not only that, but God has sent in the sum for your fares and equipment!'"

So, veteran Sam Staniford and recruit Fred Chapman sailed along the snarling West African coastline, to the "tooth" Coast (as many called the Ivory Coast), otherwise known as "the white man's grave". They launched out on a tour of investigation to the north-east of the country, along the great Comoe River, its jungled banks infested with hippos and crocodiles. Everywhere, a terrible spiritual need was revealed, with total ignorance of the Bible and of the Lord Jesus Christ.

The two pressed on even further to the north, through grassland and forest, by mountain and glen, through different tribes with diverse languages and varying customs, till they reached a tribe whom the French government officials described as "so uncivilised, so strongly attached to their fetishes and so notorious for their poisoning", that it would be impossible to grant the missionaries permits to settle there.

Into this Gourou tribal area, where 120,000 fetishers lived in superstition, witchcraft and desperate need, God called those first two intrepid Crusaders. A friendly and cheerful official eventually introduced them to the paramount chiefs of the three local tribes, saying: "These missionaries (indicating us) have come to destroy your fetishes and make you do salaams and prayers!"

From that inauspicious beginning, the work took off, and on June 3rd, 1935, the very day that Sam's wife arrived to join them, they were granted the much-prayed-for permits to take up residence among the Gourous.

1936 – Unbelief strictly prohibited!

"What is that in your hand?" asked the visitor.

"Oh," replied Alfred Ruscoe, "this is an iron. I just bought it for a quarter!"

The visitor eyed him curiously. Here was a little Englishman, recently arrived in Canada, living in one sparsely furnished room. A huge banner across the fireplace read: UNBELIEF STRICTLY PROHIBITED.

"This", he said, "is the headquarters of the Worldwide Evangelization Crusade for Canada and the United States."

Not only that, but he expected to send hundreds of young people around the world, absolutely confident that God would supply the thousands of dollars required. What a strange set-up!

Years later, when recounting this incident, Mr Ruscoe likened it to the feeding of the five thousand. "The disciples", he said, "saw only the few loaves and fishes and a vast, hungry crowd. The Lord saw the *invisible* supply." So it was with the visitor. All she could see was a little Englishman in one room who had just bought a second-hand iron for a quarter!

The real beginning had been four years earlier when Rusiko (as he was generally known) made his first visit to North America. At that time, the Lord deeply challenged him with the vision of sending young Canadian people out as missionaries, trusting God completely for the finances. The challenge continued to grow when he returned to Britain, but the more he thought and prayed about it, the more he became aware of his own inability. Completely overwhelmed by the utter impossibility of such a venture, he tried to evade it. Then, through the Scriptures, the Lord spoke to him, "Not by might nor by power, but by My Spirit, says the Lord Almighty" (Zec. 4:6). A wonderful witness of joy and peace came into his soul.

He returned to Canada, cast afresh on the faithfulness of God. So it was that in August 1936 he rented a room for eighteen dollars a month at 163 College Street, Toronto. Setting up the camp bed he had brought with him, an iron in his hand, and ten dollars in his pocket, he was in business! Little wonder that the visitor had been taken aback at the simplicity of this beginning of the Canadian branch of WEC, and the audacity of the vision.

In a very short time candidates began to apply to the mission, some for the overseas work, others for the home staff. The one room was quickly outgrown and it became necessary to take a further step of faith and rent the entire three-storey house. God honoured this, and furniture, food and finances poured in.

Then came the question: Should other headquarters be established? Feeling very burdened about the matter, Rusiko "happened" to attend a Sunday morning service at Knox Presbyterian Church in Toronto. It was Missions Sunday, and one statement stood out: "You cannot evangelise the world without a strong home base." It was the word he needed. In the three following years, he opened three new headquarters in the USA, in Charlotte, North Carolina; Seattle, Washington; and Pittsburgh, Pennsylvania.

At times, the home-base workers wondered how those overseas would be supported, if more and more were involved in home-end ministry. Also the need of the new applicants during their candidate days had to be met. The temptation grew to curtail: this led to a time of heart searching, and the Lord's assurance came to them all that they were to advance and to trust Him for *all* that would be needed.

Rusiko wrote of this decision to Norman Grubb, the British home-base director at that time, who replied: "It would be a bad landslide for your faith if from the beginning you founded your work not on faith but on the size of your bank balance!"

Before long, they outgrew No. 163. Should they look for another house? How wonderful are God's ways. A single lady in Toronto had inherited a large sum of money from her father with the condition that she should not give it away. To get around this, she purchased a thirty-three roomed "double-house" in the Rosedale area of the city, and invited WEC to occupy this new place with her. For many years until she retired, Miss Fleming was WEC's gracious hostess.

Many years had passed since those early adventures of faith, when once again the family outgrew their accommodation. The next move was to a large, beautiful home in Hamilton, Ontario where staff, candidates in training, missionaries on furlough and many visitors are still experiencing the daily grace of God, and seeing new young life thrust out to the four corners of the ever-needy harvest field of the world.

1937 – Concrete evidence

The British branch of the mission family had outgrown *their* headquarters housing capacity. Some forty-five persons – staff, candidates and guests – were packed into three adjoining houses in Highland Road, Upper Norwood. The largest room could barely accommodate everyone for meetings, and meals had to be taken in two sittings.

Leslie Sutton, in charge of the practical side of headquarters' life, had been insisting for some time that they ought to enlarge their premises, either by buying or building.

Half in fun, half seriously, Norman Grubb said: "All right, Leslie. If you've got the vision, go ahead with it."

"All right," Leslie declared, "I will!"

Three weeks later a man called, asking for some clarification about the property's boundary lines. Next door to No. 17 was a plot of land with stables at the rear. WEC rented these and had converted them into offices, unknown to the enquirer. On returning a week later, he informed Leslie, quite gratuitously, that the property next door was one of the only two remaining plots of land in the area upon which the Council would allow the erection of a building.

God was obviously moving. What would be the next move?

A few weeks later they received news of the death of an old friend of the mission, and that he had left his small house, "for use at the home end of the Crusade" plus £1,200 for its upkeep. WEC could sell the property as long as the proceeds were used for the same object.

So a plan was drawn up of the type of building they would like to erect on "the plot next door". A three-storied house, to sleep thirty, feed sixty and with a room to hold one hundred people for meetings. They were assured the cost would be about double the money currently available. The matter was laid before the Lord at the morning prayer meeting. They felt led to ask the Lord to send in men to the next candidates' training course, with such practical experience that they could be formed into a building team. This would obviate all the wages, and make it possible to erect the proposed building with the available money.

Plans had to be drawn up; materials purchased; equipment, such as scaffolding and a concrete mixer, hired. A Christian contractor, Mr Will Hopkins, was asked if he would be willing to hire or lend scaffolding. He came over to see the project. On returning home, he became sick and lay for a week in bed: there the Lord spoke to him. His business had fallen on hard times. His work-force of eighty was down to fifteen. However they had just secured a large contract.

"The hostel or the contract," God seemed to say to him.

Uncle Hoppy, as he became known, hesitated. Then he

became more seriously ill and lost the use of both of his legs.

"See how dependent you are on Me," God reminded him. "Will you give your skill and time for Me?"

Uncle Hoppy made his decision, recovered completely, and not merely loaned the scaffolding, but undertook the oversight of the whole building himself.

When the work eventually got under way in January 1937, there were twelve male candidates in the training course, among them three expert bricklayers and three excellent carpenters! During the ensuing year God sent five other specialists "just on time" as each job needed doing. Such as when 200 steel girders were delivered, and a Canadian "turned up" who had been in a building team, "erecting steel girders," before he went to Bible School.

Just when they needed to install the electric lighting system, two young electrical engineers joined the missionary candidates. Likewise, when the plumbing had to be done, two plumbers arrived to train as missionaries for West Africa and India! When the interior decoration needed to be undertaken, an Australian mission, with no English representative, approached WEC, asking them to test one of their candidates. "What was your previous job?" he was asked on arrival. His answer, of course, was "A house decorator"!

The inspector for the London County Council, watching closely for shoddy workmanship, declared he had not seen a more solid and professional job done in all his experience.

Of the twenty-six young men who took some part in the building, twenty-one went overseas in missionary service, two joined the home staff, and three returned to witness for God in their own business. "Uncle Hoppy", who had "faithfully observed to do all that the Lord had commanded him", was soon employing 200 men!

From June 1938, the "Hostel" (No. 19) was in use for the training of young men and women for the advance of the gospel in unevangelised fields, and for monthly prayer conferences for an ever-growing number of supporters.

With the "concrete evidence" of the Lord's faithfulness before them, candidates and friends learned afresh what God can do through the least of His servants who will utterly trust and obey.

1938 – Pushing back the frontiers

Into a new district in Colombia: "Since arriving here, we hardly go on to the street without speaking to someone!"

Jack and Evelyn Thomas were settling into a large new district at Honda in Colombia. "Hours have been spent in straight dealings and many are in the valley of decision. An Arab family are ever so keen. They bought a Bible and read it every day. The chief of the railway station asked us to visit his home, where we met his wife and nine children! They have offered us the use of their large drawing-room for Sunday night service and midweek Bible class. The Lord is deeply impressing them and we truly believe they will soon be in love with the Saviour."

Opening up work in Senegal: Edwy Gibbons and Leslie Brierley were just two more graduating students from Emmanuel Bible School. They had not seemed anything very special to their fellow students, just down-to-earth and basically good. Yet the next thing heard was of these two greenhorns trekking through the most inhospitable countryside in the blistering heat of West Africa searching out a resting place where they might start preaching the gospel to the sin-bound yet friendly tribesmen of Senegal.

Travelling up-country by lorry, through intense heat and tropical storms of unbelievable ferocity, they arrived at Velingara at midnight, drums throbbing all around them from a beer-dancing festival. Despite this unpromising welcome, they soon had the keys to the local "guest" house, their camp-beds up and hot cups of Bovril all round.

"Hallelujah! we are home at last!" was the triumphant entry in their diary.

There were wonderful descriptions of the insect life, and the various inhabitants in the flour, and the local public baths and drainage system, all of which left little to the imagination: but there were also deeply moving stories of cycle riding through high elephant grass along narrow ditch-like paths to reach some chieftain's village: the welcome and the hushed group who listened to the story of the crucifixion from a Fula Gospel.

"Last night we had a great meeting," Leslie's diary reads. "The hut was crowded out and there were others listening outside. I launched out into Fula and somehow managed to get through with it. They were pleased to hear, and seemed to understand what I was getting at and discussed it among themselves. Most of them agreed that there was only one way, and many said that they were going to follow the Jesus Way."

Into Liberia: "The whole history of these weeks has been one grand dovetailing of God's plans," came an excited report from New Cess. The eight new workers had been welcomed to Liberia by the Vice-President himself! They were through customs in one short hour, with next to nothing to pay. They were provided with magnificent accommodation for their three week stay in the capital, at the government's expense. What more could children of the King ask for?

As it was the farming season, they were warned that it might be impossible to hire carriers to escort them to the interior. Before they left they had all the carriers they needed! Uncertain as to where to start their ministry, they received a typewritten petition with over seventy signatures of chiefs and town-masters from the Bassa tribe, begging them to go to them with the Word of God.

From there, they were soon trekking out into the utterly untouched Gee tribal area, and again met with a great welcome from people, who almost without exception had never before heard the Name of Jesus. "I am just finishing my first Gee vocabulary," wrote Percy Clubine from Gaple, "I must get on with translating some bits of Scripture. May God give us such a great passion for these heathen souls that we must see abundant fruit."

A "chance" meeting – and so to the heart of Nepal!: Knowing nothing of Nepal or of village life, Dr Katherine Harbord had travelled alone to India, and almost turned back, as she realised the overwhelming nature of the dangers and difficulties ahead.

"God told me," she had written, from a remote town on the border of Nepal, "that He had never promised us safety in His service; there is no promise of being kept from sickness, death or worse: but He has promised to bring us victoriously through such trials. I have faced every possibility I can think of, and I know now that whatever happens, the very worst I can think of, still I can never doubt Him. He may allow every evil to touch my body, but I am still His, and by His grace I shall praise Him all through!"

No wonder she triumphed when struck down, first with cholera and then with smallpox, during epidemic outbreaks in the region! She stuck it out, and then God honoured her triumphant faith in a truly remarkable way. He brought her right into the capital of Nepal, through a "chance" meeting with a government agent. "He asked who I was, and taking my name and degrees said: 'No doubt the governor will require the services of a lady doctor to attend his ladies'!" Within three months, she had been called to attend the governor's daughter in her confinement – and spent two whole months right in "closed" Nepal!

In the heart of Kashmir: "Our eyes have been opened wide to the awful need of this untouched district," wrote Arthur Downing from the heart of Kashmir. "The little dispensary we opened, with such simple medicines as we know how to use, has been such a boon! Many doors and hearts have been opened. We have had hearty invitations to the untouched regions of Bhardawah, Kishtawar, Kathua and Mirpur, each with over 200,000 souls for whom Christ died; and that from the leading government officials as well as the poor people. Oh, for more helpers!"

1939 – "Mungu iko!"

"It is really a wonder, that we have been so long without this," wrote Ena Bush in 1937, as she inaugurated a young people's branch of WEC. "We have always realised when reading letters from the fields, that the experiences of our Crusaders as they tramp in search of souls through dark forest and over lofty mountain ranges – meeting fierce animals and often fiercer men in the world's remotest corners – are the very stuff to enthral the youngsters.

"Does the boy feel in his blood the call of the wild? Here it is, in the Himalayas or the Congo forest. Is the girl moved with pity for the suffering? There they are in their millions, the leprous, the outcast, the orphan."

Ena Bush (later to marry William Pethybridge) had a good position in the Intelligence Department of Barclays Bank, but was called to resign her post and join WEC headquarters staff, despite every effort to put her off!

She had a love for young people, a bent for writing, and a varied business training. And, in a very short time, by her enthusiasm and vision, was born the "Young Warriors" (YW). Members were grouped in bands, and greeted one another with a peculiar African handshake coupled with their war cry: *Mungu iko*! (God is.)

By 1938, the YW's had taken off! Bands were being formed all over the United Kingdom, each attached to a special field, with its own "Front Line Warrior". Leaders were excited at the possibilities of building young Christians up with a real missionary interest. Almost every day, Ena received news of conversions in the Bands, and splendid

answers to prayer, with Young Warriors witnessing boldly
for Christ in school and open air. Parcels of hand-made
gifts, knitted jerseys and bandages, "wordless" books, and
a variety of food-stuffs were going all over the world and
being greatly appreciated.

During 1939, Norman Grubb was busily touring the United
States of America with Fred Anthony. The WEC had long
desired to establish a headquarters in the USA but were
awaiting God's exact timing.

It had come! Dr and Mrs Henry Woods had published a
gift edition of *C. T. Studd* for American students. Ten years
before, they had published the life of Hudson Taylor,
which had been instrumental in calling out 200 students for
China. Now they wanted to "see God do it again" and
invited Norman Grubb to tour the universities and challenge young life with worldwide missionary vision.

"The result has been overwhelming!" Norman wrote.
They took 600 meetings in universities, Bible Schools and
churches, covering 14,000 miles. Hundreds of new contacts
were made, and invitations from all sides to "come again"!
Yet this was only the background to the real objective of
opening a Mission Headquarters in the USA, "from which
an army of young people can march out to the unevangelised parts of the world."

Suddenly things began to crystallise. A pressing invitation to visit a lady in Charlotte (North Carolina), a dinner
party, meeting a leader of the Christian Business Men's
Organisation, an urgent call to Rusiko (Alfred Ruscoe) to
"come south [from the WEC headquarters in Toronto] and
see for himself".

When Rusiko arrived, a public welcome was arranged,
and the local newspaper had a column on its front page on
the coming of WEC to their city!

God gave them a double-fronted house of red brick on a
hill, with half an acre of land, plus a large garage. There
were ten big rooms and large attic space. It was ideal. And

the Lord had so touched the hearts of His people in North Carolina that the rent and heating costs were all underwritten, as was the usual commission on purchase.

Rusiko "took possession" with one candidate, and the two of them scrubbed and decorated from top to toe. Reba Fleming was called by God from Toronto, to be House Mother at the Charlotte Headquarters. Then followed remarkable stories month after month of the provision of all needed furniture and household goods. Before the year was out, not only were there three staff members and two candidates at the Charlotte Headquarters, but they were busy opening another headquarters in the west.

It was a trial of faith for Rusiko. The exchequer was very low: no more American volunteers had yet been called to work at the home-end. "It seemed madness," he wrote, "and against my better judgment and common sense, but I just seemed compelled to obey." He had set out on the 3,000 mile journey west with nothing but his rail fare. En route, he stopped off to attend a "Victorious Life Conference" in Minneapolis. Here the Lord poured out blessing in a way he had never experienced before, hundreds of people having their lives blessed. From among these, two couples were called by God for full-time service at the home-end of WEC!

When he eventually reached Seattle, forty gathered for a prayer meeting. Then Rusiko was led to a nine-roomed frame house on Capitol Hill . . . and in less time than it takes to tell, the house was theirs, plus furnishings "thrown in"! Arthur and Lilian Davidson took charge, in preparation for their return to New Zealand to open a headquarters there.

And, during the *same* year, the Young Warriors were launched in the United States. Ethel Rodway had set out for Liberia, but her health made it impossible. In England, she had spent time with Ena Bush, and came back to the States "sold out" for the Youth Programme, ready to cry

"*Mungu iko!*" from east to west of the vast country, and so to mobilise young people for the Crusade.

1940 – "Alone, yet not alone"

Bessie, "a fair-haired blue-eyed scrap of humanity", used to forage round the market stalls late in the evenings, looking for damaged vegetables at give-away prices or some scrag-ends of meat to help feed the six hungry mouths at home in London's East End.

Bessie loved "Arthur's Mission" in Bermondsey as somewhere to go on Sundays. The youngsters may have appeared rough and shabby, but appearances didn't matter there. Loving and caring were the priorities. Bessie, like the rest, would swear, pilfer and indulge in fisticuffs, and it took four years' regular Bible teaching to bring her to the place of giving herself to the Lord Jesus Christ, who had so loved her as to die for her. She could not have explained in theological terms what had happened to her, but God recorded the transaction in heaven, and from that moment Bessie knew that her life was no longer to be lived for herself, but in obedience to Him, who had redeemed her.

Challenged for the mission field, Bessie believed the proposition was impossible. That God should ever want her, poor uneducated Bessie Fricker, for the mission field, was an incredible thought! But the members of Arthur's Mission backed her, and sent her off to Bible School.

"Why, to be in Bible School and to be able to study the Bible for three whole years – that must be heaven on earth!" day-dreamed Bessie.

Rude awakening came as she tackled an intelligence assessment test the first day. Her failure was so complete that she was sure she would be turned out! But God had called her . . . Fortunately her tutors recognised this, and she stayed.

"Such a lot of stuff they make you learn here," she used

to say, "far above my poor brains. Psychology and ethics . . . I hardly understand a word!"

However, she plodded on with dogged determination, until her name appeared among the top three students on the examination lists. "I did my best, and He made me a sticker!" she commented drily, giving all the glory to God.

Norman Grubb came regularly to the School, laying before the students the world's needs, the vast areas of each continent not yet penetrated by the Christian messenger.

"You don't go to the mission field if you can help it, but, if the Lord has called you, you can't help it!" – so spoke the visiting missionary, and Bessie *knew* that God had called her to an unevangelised region in West Africa, to serve with WEC. After much prayer, she was convinced that God wanted her in Portuguese Guinea. The mission had no work there as yet, but agreed to her going to Angola first to gain experience and get to grips with the language. Throughout her three years there, her heart was yearning for Portuguese Guinea.

There seemed to be endless set-backs and hindrances. First one plan was suggested, and then another. Three young men were to go first in preparation, and she would follow. Then one of these became so ill, it seemed he would never be able to go. Correspondence with England was desperately slow. Most frustrating of all to Bessie was that, being a woman, she was not allowed to go with the advance party!

Eventually, permission was granted for Bessie and the three men to leave Angola and sail for the Cape Verde Islands, from where the men could more easily enter the "promised land". Then the shattering news arrived – having sailed for Portuguese Guinea, the men were beating a retreat, because they had not enough funds to build to the government's standards!

"You can imagine what a shock this was to me. I wept and wept when I received the letter. I fasted and prayed and pleaded with the Lord to help them not to leave."

Then came a telegram announcing the *resignation* of the three.

"I thought my heart would break. I cannot describe what it means to me."

As Bessie fought a lonely battle amidst a multitude of suggestions and counter-suggestions, the decision of her life was made – she would *not* leave WEC, and she *would* go into Portuguese Guinea, even if alone. Everything was against her – her inability with the language and to deal with government papers; the impossibility of a woman living alone; the question of leadership – "but I know that God can look after me, and will; all that matters is to do His Will."

After pressing the home staff for a favourable and quick decision, she was delighted when the cable came: "Enter Guinea before rains!" In two weeks she was on her way. "I can hardly believe it is true. *Never* did I need prayer more than I do now," she wrote home. "So don't fail. I go alone, yet *not alone* – with Him!"

May 20th, 1940, she arrived and opened the WEC ministry in Portuguese Guinea. With God, indeed, all things are possible!

1941 – From "EPH" to "CLC"

"The increasing stress put by Christian leaders upon the vast worldwide need of Christian literature makes us realise more than ever," reported WEC personnel who had become deeply involved in a new venture called the Evangelical Publishing House (EPH), "that God has been in the founding of this new literature branch of WEC."

"Few people realise that over one thousand million people, now illiterate, will probably become literate during this century." So read a leaflet published by Edinburgh House. "There is a worldwide movement for literacy. Millions will soon be reading. The Christian Church must work out a new strategy for supplying the world with good books.''

The month after that statement had been published, November 1st, 1941, WEC called a meeting of the sixteen workers of its Evangelical Publishing House, from its six book centres up and down the UK, along with four leaders from other departments of the WEC home-end staff, to be held in the Colchester bookshop.

By far the most important conviction borne in upon everyone at that conference was that God had called the EPH into being for something much larger than merely opening a number of book centres in Christian countries and using profits for the general help of evangelical work. God fired them to see the urgent need of bringing to birth a *Christian Literature Crusade*, devoted solely to the work of spreading pure evangelical literature all over the world.

This vision was no man-planned affair. The EPH had started in great weakness, with Ken and Bessie Adams turning an upstairs room in that Colchester house into a bookroom. Then Christians in many English towns, and later in Toronto, Canada, and then Sydney, Australia, had approached the team and *asked* for evangelical bookshops to be opened in their areas. So in the absence of any strictly evangelical agency, responsible for spreading spiritual literature wholly true to God's Word, the group came to a unanimous agreement to launch this new branch of WEC. It was to link up and serve the many colporteurs and local mission book agencies, and to establish bookshops as centres of living witness and Christian fellowship.

Information was gathered from all Bible and missionary societies and booksellers' organisations, and a large wall-map prepared showing the location of all existing Christian presses and outlets for Christian literature. Plans were made for the translation, printing, publishing and distributing of the much needed literature, and for sending out specially trained "CLC" personnel (within the ranks of WEC) to open up the necessary new outlets.

All the workers of the new Crusade would be selected,

tested and accepted into the ranks alongside all other WEC candidates, and all would agree to accept no salary or allowance, but to look to God alone to supply their needs.

Within two months of its birth, the new Christian Literature Crusade had urgent calls from North Africa, North India, Colombia and Peru in South America, and Senegal in West Africa. Arthur Downing was prepared to start a book centre in Srinagar (Kashmir), and Pat Symes in the centre of Bogota, Colombia. A book store in St Louis in Senegal was suggested as the only means of contacting Maures from the closed land of Mauritania. Mr McNairn of the EUSA Mission was prepared to start a shop in the centre of Lima, Peru, if CLC could provide a worker to assist him.

A Bureau of Information on evangelical literature in foreign languages was started. A library of all available translations of evangelical books was set up in the new CLC headquarters in London. Mobile literature units were developed both for the home work and for abroad, to sleep four and equipped with loudspeakers for open air ministry.

The launching of "Floodtide", the bi-monthly magazine of CLC, was another exciting new move in the history of the Crusade. "It has a magnificent ideal before it," said the first editorial, "news, needs and developments of evangelical literature throughout the world." Through its challenging pages, the Christian public were continually reminded of the need for personnel for book centres in ever increasing numbers of countries.

Today the Christian Literature Crusade, a fully fledged mission in its own right, still linked to WEC for fellowship, has almost one hundred missionary workers and nearly five hundred national workers in 130 book centres in forty countries around the world, bringing light and encouragement and challenge to millions.

1942 – "When are you coming again?"

The Seamans were tremendously conscious of God's helping hand, as they ploughed through all the difficulties of
entry into Gold Coast (now Ghana), with the problems of
currency exchanges and finding living accommodation.
With the initial welcome of people and officials ringing in
their ears, they pioneered up into the far north-western
corner of the country through rain and mud, splashing
through swollen rivers, shoving and heaving the heavily
laden car out of ruts and ditches, to arrive at their first
chosen centre of Kani.

"The Lord has definitely brought us into this land," Edna
wrote, "and He will supply our every need and bring many
souls to Himself. It is wonderful to realise that God has
brought us into this promised land at a time when advance
work, humanly speaking, would not seem possible; but we
are rejoicing in a loving Father whose plans are not dependent on world conditions, whose authority is not determined by the rise and fall of empires, but His promises are
yea and amen, and whose supplies never fail!"

The acting District Commissioner was a tremendous help
and encouragement to them, advising about the choice of
site for the first church centre at Tuna, among the Gonja
tribes-people. "I wish you could have seen him and
ourselves scrambling through eight foot high grass, climbing trees and wading through water in order to find us the
most suitable location."

"We already have the bricks made," came an excited
letter, a month later. "They weigh over six kilos each: and
after loading and unloading for some time, I had great
difficulty in sitting down, and even greater in getting up!"

The two missionaries already spoke Lobi from a period
of time spent in Ivory Coast: now they settled down, one to
learn Gonja and the other Wala. As soon as they had a
smattering of each, they were out in the villages and talking
with the folk, telling them about Jesus, who is the Light of
the World, whom God sent to dispel man's darkness and

ignorance, and to overcome his sin and failures. Crowds gathered each time, delighted to hear new truths in their own mother tongue.

When in the local township of Kumasi for needed stores and building material, the two saw a tandem bicycle, offered at a ludicrously cheap price. So they set off for home on "Hurricane Bronco", followed by the amused stares of every African they passed! Lumps of rock and hidden tree stumps set an obstacle race along the rough forest track, yet only one of a bowl of precious eggs, given them by a grateful chieftain en route, got smashed before arriving home!

"The folk have realised we are here to help them. The chief asked me to see an old man who has been ill for a month. Within four visits, he began to improve. A woman with bad eyes has been cured. If only we had a nurse with us! There are wide open doors here. Where are the soldiers? We can accomplish nothing in our own strength, but by God's power much will be done."

Next month, Edna continued the saga of the building of their home. "While Leslie has been doing window frames, I have built the granite and stone wall round the front of the verandah. It looks posh! I little realised when I watched the Hostel at London Headquarters being put up, that I should one day be laying bricks in Africa. The villagers here are watching to see what will happen – 'What will these two achieve, with a war on?' Europeans are even more surprised, especially to see a woman on the job!"

Don Theobald arrived the following year, and was filled with admiration for the Seamans. "They have won the confidence of all the local folk, villagers and chieftains and administrators alike. They have opened wide a door for the preaching of the gospel, and made an impressive start on four of the necessary languages. We are surrounded by a vast area of need, with at least seven tribal groups, centred on 200 large villages. We would need at least a week in each to make any lasting impression, and that means that we would only get round them all once in four years! As half the country is only open in the dry season, we must open up work in the other half so that they too can hear the good news."

"The building of the centre has been a glorious experience," Edna adds, as they and the local people had learned to trust and respect and love each other, "but we are now having a far greater thrill. The people have *asked* us to go every evening to tell them God's Word. The chief has said they want to finish with all their witchcraft and 'follow God's way', which they have seen is much better. Oh, hasn't it been worth building with bricks that we might have this infinite joy of building with lives!"

The three trekked right across the Gonja district, sleeping in a different village each night, preaching the Word to a different crowd each day. "Oh, if you could get a vision of the great need out here," they wrote home, "of chains of witchcraft and superstition which bind them to Satan, and yet their willingness to hear the gospel, surely some would be constrained for the love of Christ to lay down their lives for the salvation of 100,000 Gonjas!"

Everywhere, along every road, there was the same openness to hear the gospel and to be rid of their fetishes; but no one was there to teach and establish them. "When are you coming again?" they were asked each day. Maybe not for four years. "How can we say that to them in the same breath as telling them that God loves them?"

1943 – Faith knows nothing of retreat

"Thirty years old – and how much nearer are we to our God-given goal than when we started out?" mused Norman Grubb, as he looked out on vast regions as yet completely unreached with the gospel. "This mission came into being as an *army* to conquer the world for Christ. Let each missionary, called and chosen and faithful, stand to arms and play the man!

"Faith knows nothing of retreat," he challenged his

troops. "The devil is a defeated foe. The bitter cry of unsaved millions, 'Come over and help us,' is only less powerful than the thrilling command of the Lord Jesus Christ, 'Go into all the world and preach the good news to all creation.' Unreached tribes, unevangelised areas, closed lands – we face them bravely in the power of the Spirit, and with faith, prayer, love and sacrifice."

A tremendous world survey was undertaken during the year to identify the remaining unreached areas and peoples, and figures began to bombard the Christian public demanding meaningful prayer and appropriating faith for a moving forward towards the mission's declared goal.

"Three hundred million benighted in superstition-ridden Confucianism: 210 million steeped in the grovelling idolatry of Hinduism: 230 million crowding the sorrowful temples of Buddha: 220 million in the ugly grip of fanatical Islam: 158 million groping in the fear-haunted darkness of animism and fetishism" and so on and so on ". . . and millions without number nurtured, trained, lost and perishing in the cold, futile atmosphere of dialectical materialism, political delusion and Christ-crucifying secularism." Is it nothing to you . . . ?

A gigantic task waiting to be tackled . . . and a mighty God, a mighty gospel, a mighty power to tackle it. "Greater is He that is with you than he that is in the world," Norman Grubb reminded his troops.

Leslie Brierley, now married to Bessie Fricker of Portuguese Guinea, came home on furlough from Senegal with devastating and accurate details of the task remaining to be done in West Africa. This both humbled the mission for past failure, and stimulated them for future effort.

20 areas in Western West Africa; 5 million unreached
20 areas in Central West Africa; 12 million unreached
6 areas in Southern West Africa; 1 million unreached
6 areas in Central and East Africa; 3 million unreached
7 areas in North East Africa; over 2 million unreached

The message flashed out in bold print: "NEEDED: 150 pioneers for final advance in Africa," and a clear statement of what would make an applicant suitable.

Leslie then turned his attention to India's enormous problems, and broke the statistics down so that everyone could begin to grasp the size of the need.

In north-east, 36 million; less than 2 workers/million
In north-west, 27 million; less than 2 workers/million

"In Central Asia, Afghanistan, Russian Turkestan, Mongolia, Tibet, Nepal, Bhutan (all closed) – 17 million in the fanatically Muslim group: 30 million in the Soviet group: and 12 million in the Buddhist group. All waiting to hear."

South-east Asia was similarly surveyed, where 20 million waited to be reached in Indo-China and Thailand, as yet outside the programme of any other mission. Maps were prepared and published with unreached areas blocked in in black. A twenty-seven-field programme was prepared as the immediate challenge to the Crusade, and a ringing communiqué published.

"Under the urge of the Spirit, we can take no rest ourselves, nor give His people rest, nor give Him rest (Isaiah 62:7) until these twenty-seven named unevangelised fields are adequately occupied by a chain of centres which gives each tribe or group of peoples in them a chance to hear of Christ."

To support this enormous challenge for advance overseas, it was essential to strengthen all the home bases and speed up the selection and training of candidates suitable for such pioneering. In Canada, the United States of America, Australia, New Zealand and the United Kingdom, nationwide campaigns of challenge were planned and prayed over, the two crystal-clear emphases of every meeting to be (1) on inner cleansing, and (2) on outer action, a life of service in the power of the Holy Spirit.

One Australian missionary, on furlough from Colombia, recorded how deeply impressed he was during the campaign by "the numbers of keen young people who are going through with God and facing up to the challenge of Christ and the mission field. C. T. Studd's life still bowls them over like nine-pins," he declared. "University students, church members, young peoples' fellowships, all seem to respond to the challenge of C. T.'s consecrated life."

1944 – The God of the Impossible!

The departure of Henry Tyskerud from Canada to India was so obviously impossible that the Toronto Headquarters' family were still wondering, a month after the event, if the string of miracles which extended for five days before their eyes actually happened, or would later be proved to be a dream. Let them tell the story in their own words.

"It began on Thursday, May 18th. A well-known shipping company phoned to say that a passage to India had been booked for Henry for Tuesday, May 23rd. For a few minutes we sat, stunned. Finally someone asked: 'How much of your outfit have you, Henry?' and the answer was: 'A sleeping bag and a typewriter.' Then, 'How much money have you towards your passage and outfit?' (At least 1,200 Canadian dollars would be needed.) The laconic answer: 'Thirty-eight dollars and thirteen cents.'

"So we sat and looked at each other. Even if the money had been on hand, the task of buying an outfit would have been almost impossible in so short a time. The tea chests required for packing must be procured, cut in halves, painted, have lids made, and be addressed with brush and paint. Then time was needed for the packing and listing of all the items.

"It wasn't the outfit alone, however, that gave us concern. Henry's passport could not be validated without permission from India and it had taken a month to get the previous one done. How could we get it in time for Ottawa to take action by Saturday morning, which they must do if the passport were to reach Toronto by Monday? There were injections, dental work, travellers' cheques . . . and so the mountains grew.

"As we talked the matter over and realised the impossibility of the situation, two facts stood out. The first was that Mr Gillman would not have booked the passage in New York if he had not had definite guidance from God. The second was that we were dealing with *the God of the Impossible*. As we took this stand, the Lord gave faith to us and from that time on we were unanimous in the assurance that Henry would sail on the day appointed.

"Having reached this point, we drew up a plan of action. One was sent to phone to the government in Ottawa, with the request that they cable India for the necessary permission. While another went to the files for the outfit list, others went and rummaged through drawers and boxes, and gave Henry an impromptu 'birthday party' – towels, bedding, socks, pillow-slips, shoes, and a good suit of clothes – nor were the partially completed outfits of other candidates spared!

"The remaining needs for his outfit were divided into several sections, and a dozen people started off to do Henry's shopping. Some of the boys went to work on the boxes. From Thursday noon to Tuesday morning there was not a dull or idle moment for anyone in the family.

"To anyone not used to seeing the Lord supply, without appeals made or needs advertised, the way the money showered in would appear unbelievable. It just seemed to come from everywhere. Telegrams from Philadelphia and Charlotte brought 350 dollars. When Henry said goodbye in his home town, they loaded him down with many gifts for his outfit, and 240 dollars in cash. This was in addition to the many gifts received in Toronto.

"While Henry was in town, others packed his boxes. When he arrived in India, he would see much of his outfit for the first time! But the outstanding matters were the passport and exit permit from the Selective Service Board. Unbelievably, the passport arrived by special airmail delivery on Saturday, just two days after the request was made. The Selective Service permit had been overlooked because Henry's exemption was thought to be sufficient. However, late on Monday afternoon it was discovered that it was necessary, and the Board was applied to within an hour of closing time.

"The man in charge said that this permission must come from Ottawa, and it would be absolutely impossible for Henry to leave the next morning. Mr Gunn explained to him that we were Christians, and that we believed that it was the Lord's will for Henry to leave on the morning train. The official asked: 'Do you believe in miracles?' to which Mr Gunn replied, 'We certainly do!' 'Well, now is the time to get one, for this boy will never leave tomorrow morning.' He then wrote out the name of the man in Ottawa authorised to grant this permit. Mr Gunn was astonished to find the name was that of a man whom he had met in Ottawa a few days previously.

"When the phone call was made Tuesday morning, the exit permit was very graciously granted and forwarded from Ottawa to the seaport from which Henry was to sail. Henry had actually left before the phone call was made, being well assured that the God who had already removed many other obstacles, would also remove this one!

"So once again, the Toronto Union Station rang with hymns as a large circle of Crusaders and friends gathered to wish him Godspeed."

1945 – "I don't want to go to heaven now!"

"I don't want to go to heaven now," said a young hopeful, aged four, to his mother. "I want to stay at the Elms."

How immeasurably easier the parting was made for this mother, as she returned without her children to her work in Africa.

For several years, WEC had been waiting on God concerning the needs of their growing family of children. "We knew that whatever the Lord led us to do for the children," the committee declared in faith, "we could be quite sure that He would do in bountiful fashion, so that, as the children grew up, they would be able to see for themselves the faithfulness of the Heavenly Father in whom their parents had trusted."

Correspondence with all on the fields, discussions with all who came on furlough, over a period of several years, led to a firm conviction that the choice would be a home in the homeland rather than school on the field, as had been originally thought. Then, during 1942, Charlie and Lily Searle, two ex-Congo missionaries, who could not return to the field for health reasons, but who were both specially gifted with children, realised that God was speaking to them, each of them individually, about this urgent need. And so, in January 1945, the two of them offered themselves for service in a children's home. Step one was thus achieved.

Through a passing remark, made really as a joke, the next move took place. A co-worker at the Aberdeen Headquarters commented that she knew a wonderful estate then being used by Polish officers, which would "be just the thing for a children's home!" It was on the outskirts of Arbroath, a little seaside resort on the east coast of Scotland.

"The Elms" was a fine stone-built mansion of the last century, standing in three acres of woodland, with several large rooms, a conservatory and a good kitchen on the ground floor and fourteen bedrooms on the first floor, plus out-houses which could easily be turned into extra bedrooms. Further enquiries discovered that the owner was willing to sell, and at a very reasonable price!

Several members of the home staff went on a tour of inspection – it sounded almost too good to be true! Only half an hour's walk from the seaside, it was also within five minutes' walk of the excellent local primary school and fifteen minutes' from the High School.

All seemed ideal, with the one exception of the money

with which to purchase it. Then, in the early months of 1945, the mission received a large gift of £5,000 specifically designated for the purchase of a Missionary Children's Home. After careful negotiations, "The Elms" was bought for £3,100, the balance of money being used for the installation of central heating and the purchase of necessary furnishings. Step two had been achieved.

Another couple were called by God at the same time, Stephen Cottam to help in the gardens and with the unending practical jobs that would need doing, and his wife, a gold-medallist nurse, experienced in the care of sick children, to care for the health of the children. Other single ladies applied, to help with sewing and domestic jobs.

By the close of the year, all was completed, and they were in! Step three had been achieved.

"Pray for us!" wrote Charlie Searle. "This is only the beginning, not the end. We aim to train the children for the Master, that they in their turn may reveal Him to a needy world."

Then came letter after letter telling of amazing things that God was doing for them. One lovely example was how God chose to supply the need of teaspoons. "The Lord supplied us with cutlery which was in very short supply. We received knives, forks, dessert and tablespoons, but no teaspoons. Why the apparent lack? Then Stephen pointed out to me", Charlie wrote, "a blocked drain. He kneeled down, and pulled out some large pieces of old rag, and then . . . a teaspoon? No! forty-six teaspoons! The Lord provided Peter's tax money out of the mouth of a fish: and our teaspoons out of a drain!"

Stephen himself also wrote telling of some of the remarkable answers to prayer . . . the arrival of a potato-peeling machine, a dozen beds and mattresses, a bread-cutting machine that looked more like a bacon slicer, a can opener . . . and so on and so on. A Christian farmer provided a brand-new bicycle. A lady asked for the names and birthdays of each child in the home so as to send them a small gift on the right day.

They needed a plumber, an electrician, a carpenter and a decorator. They were all praying for a piano and a piano teacher . . . and both came within the month! Then a handy-man "turned up", willing to stay three months and do all he could. Someone else "found a load of glass that he didn't need" and the greenhouses were duly repaired! The list of God's abundant supplies never seemed to end.

"Pray with us", was the deep heart-cry from all the staff, "that each child will come to know for him or herself, this wonderful Saviour who has poured all this goodness upon us."

1946 – Called, chosen, faithful

Letters poured in from all over the world, as the news spread rapidly: "Harri glorified – May 7th."

Just forty-five years old, in the prime of life, Jack Harrison had been the Congo Field Leader for only four-teen years, when his untimely death, humanly speaking, occurred.

Norman Grubb spoke of the "stunning shock. His place in WEC has been unique: no one person can replace him. He had been like a son to C. T. and had drunk deep of his spirit, and lived, almost as completely as any man could live, for Jesus. His life preached more loudly than any words, and kept pointing us, like a true compass, to the standards of faith and sacrifice and complete devotion to Christ and souls, upon which WEC was founded. For myself, he was a constant living inspiration and silent challenge."

"We do all praise God for every remembrance of Jack and the way he went all out for God," wrote Jack Scholes, his closest friend in the Congo. "We came through colony-training days together, sailed for the field together, and have worked closely in harmony together these twenty-five years. His loving friendship has meant more to me than I can ever say."

"What a shock!" wrote Edith Moules, who only three

years previously had lost her own husband out in the Congo. "As a brother he was loved by all," she continued. "As a missionary, his life was a challenge – spiritually, he was ever on the stretch for the highest. As a leader, he was an inspiration, with unswerving determination and no compromise."

"His life has been a tremendous inspiration to me," wrote another colleague, who had known him since colony-training days. "One has just marvelled at his growth in grace and the way he shouldered his heavy responsibilities. He was a brave soldier of the Cross and his one passion was the salvation of souls and the extension of Christ's kingdom. We have lost not only a leader, but a man of God from our midst, who loved the Word and the secret place of prayer. He burnt himself out for love of God and the salvation of precious souls."

"Truly Jack proved himself a leader of God's choice," Esme Roupell wrote. "A man who ceased not to wait upon God for guidance and then fearlessly went forward."

Jack Harrison, the successor to C. T. Studd of Eton and Cambridge, was born in Liverpool in a humble home, with no special advantages. At the local school he was popular among boys and teachers, bright and keen, always top of his class. He started work in the wine and bottling trade at the age of thirteen, whilst, in a back-garden shed, he carried on his leisure work of mending broken things and making stopped watches go, of cutting out fret-work toys and leading a local orchestra with piano accordion or tin whistle! He regularly attended a Sunday School in the "cathedral up the alley" under the leadership of John Wesley Arnold and eventually, as an eighteen year old, accepted Christ on Armistice Day 1918.

He never looked back. He fed voraciously upon the Word, he sought to obey all he learned, and he hated compromise. His stand cost him his friends, and soon afterwards, his job. Jack had become a person of one purpose – to know God, and His will. He was introduced by his minister to "a home for stray cats and dogs that is now being cleaned and made ready for a training centre for missionaries" – the future colony! Jack packed and left for London with ten pounds in his pocket.

One night, when on holiday in Liverpool and visiting the home of his old minister, burdened by the aimlessness of his life, he joined the family for evening prayers. The youngest child, Bronwen, aged about three, prayed: "God bless the little black boys in Africa, and send someone quickly to tell them about Jesus" and God sealed His word into Jack's heart as his life's call. He sailed in 1922, and wrote to his mother: "Do pray much, Mother, that God might use me to His glory. Out here, He needs labourers, co-workers, fellow-sufferers. Ask that I might be made usable, whatever the cost; pliable to His will in all things. The responsibility is so great, the calling so high, the honour so tremendous, that it needs an army of praying ones to keep one man out here really true, really separated unto the gospel, really prayerful and on top."

Then started nine years of hard apprenticeship, while the far-sighted C. T. trained him for future leadership. Instead of being the fiery evangelist that he had felt called to be, he became a mere handyman at the beck and call of everyone, sharpening knives and scissors, and repairing boots and watches. A fire of resentment began to rage inside him, becoming "a veritable tornado until even sleep went from me".

Planning to tell C. T. that he had not come to Africa to do odd jobs but to preach the gospel, God spoke to him, through the message of the angel to Hagar. "Where are you going? Return and submit." Jack gave in. A missionary asked him one day soon after, as he was putting in the last nail in a pair of boots: "How is it that you do all these odd jobs for us?" He replied with gusto: "I do it all for Jesus – Hallelujah!"

1947 – "Who is my neighbour?"

"One evening at the dispensary, after a hard day's work," wrote Edith Patten, "I suddenly saw him." At the back of all the other patients, he had been standing there unobserved for a time . . . he had leprosy. He was terribly mutilated, almost naked, his toes and fingers gone, his feet swollen, no nose, and dribbling from his lipless mouth down over his bare body.

That evening in 1939, every argument in the book came to her mind as to why it was impossible for her to treat this man – contagion, public opinion, no drugs available. Then he came, hobbling across to her, led by a small boy. "We have come to come," he said simply, using an African idiom. The young boy looked up at her wistfully. "We have come from beyond Poko," the child whispered – over one hundred miles, through the forest, on those feet.

Edith wanted to say "No, God – I am not here to treat their sicknesses, but to preach the gospel," but during the next four days of inner struggle, God told her clearly that that was a shibboleth.

That night, she gave the two shelter in a tumble-down shack, and some food from the communal gardens that cost her nothing. Tomorrow, they were there again, with the other 300 patients at the clinic.

"I had nothing to give him. I didn't want to touch him. There was an awful shrinking in my heart towards him. I told God I was sorry for him, but it was not my job. I argued for four days. I was supposedly in prayer before God, but that was not the true agony of prayer, for true intercession dies for its objective. God was trying to talk to me, and I was trying not to listen.

"On the fourth evening, God brought to my mind the story of the Good Samaritan, and the man who quibbled as to who was his neighbour – just as I was doing," Edith admitted. "Jesus showed me that night who my neighbour was. And I was to love him as myself, whatever he looked like or smelt like.

"Next day, I tried to tell the man and the boy that Jesus had told me to love them with His love. We knelt down together, the man with the swollen feet, the little boy with the wistful face, and this queer woman with the white hair. And we talked to our heavenly Father, and they said: Amen."

That was the beginning.

"You can't imagine their condition, those poor sufferers from earth's vilest disease," wrote Edith Patten in January of 1940. So the work of caring for, loving and treating these outcasts of society had begun. Intravenous chaulmoogra oil was used at first. Every clinic, to which these poor sufferers streamed in ever increasing numbers, always started with prayers and teaching from the Word of God. Slowly Christian communities grew up in the camps, churches were built, and *hope* entered, where before all had been despair.

September 1940: "102 new cases have presented themselves for treatment at Paku, where there are now over 300 patients. A Red Cross doctor has examined the first 150 after six months intensive treatment, and reports 40 per cent amelioration, for which we praise God."

At Atakobo, a camp of several hundred, a new church had been built to seat 200: at Pawa, where there were nearly a thousand patients, there was a keen group of Christians: at Bengwe, thirty miles east, 150 came to the services.

"Lately," Edith reported, "we have visited four large segregation camps with the Government Doctor. There are 750 leprosy patients for whom practically nothing is being done. Yesterday, we went fifty miles to another centre, where we found forty patients in a most pitiable state, mutilated and with untended wounds."

In November 1940, Edith married Percy Moules, the ideal partner for her. Humble, gentle, Christlike, thoroughly reliable; he was Edith's complement. If she was brilliant, he was durable. Together they laid their burden for the leprosy patients before the Lord, and saw the need for a central camp, available to all sufferers within the WEC area of responsibility.

June 1941: "Our hearts are full of praise, for the Red Cross has approached us to take charge of the camp at Mabese, where there are 400 patients." They were granted a small concession near the camp, Nebobongo, where they built their own home and a centre for caring for the clean children of leprous parents – all within seven miles of Ibambi, the administrative centre of WEC work.

Through the next five years, every WEC magazine had reports of the growing work, the ever-increasing number of patients receiving treatment, the churches springing up in every camp and the training of leprosy sufferers as evangelists. In 1943, they mentioned that they then had over one thousand in their care, and that the first thirty-three had been discharged symptom free, amidst great rejoicing!

In October 1944, Edith's husband, Percy, died of typhoid. Her heart crushed and almost broken, she rose above her personal tragedy, and poured herself even more than previously, if that were possible, into the care of these sufferers. And by 1947, a vision that had been growing in her heart, came into being. The *Leprosy and Medical Crusade* (LMC) was born within the ranks of WEC, to give medical care to *all* needy people in all places around the world where the Crusade worked.

1948 – Three miles high

"I had just passed my eighteenth birthday," wrote Len Moules, brother of Edith's husband Percy. "Life in the factory had tested my religious faith and found it wanting. A flood of blasphemy, foul-mouthed workmen, filthy and suggestive talk poured their constant daily contribution into my young and fertile mind. I staggered before its impact, lost my footing and was swept down its damning course."

Then a crisis occurred. Finding a Christian workman by the bench, Len poured out his troubles – a tainted mind, breaking faith, a discredited Bible and nowhere to turn. This faithful man sat down with Len over their lunchtime sandwiches and an open Bible.

"I realised that I would always need Someone", Len recorded, "to help me fight my spiritual battles." He knew the answer was to allow the Saviour to live in him and to run his life. "There and then I gave to God all that there was of me, and from that moment I was under entirely new management."

Inspired by the testimonies of Mildred Cable and Doggett Learner of the China Inland Mission, he developed a great interest in Tibet. In 1933, he left home for Bible College. Looking for a missionary society in whose ranks he could get to work amongst the Tibetans, Len met Norman Grubb, and was encouraged to apply to WEC. His long-time admirer, Iris Smith, came to know Christ as her Saviour during 1934, and became his fiancée in July 1935.

On November 30th, 1936, Len and Iris faced a separation of undetermined length. The next day Len sailed for India. Crossing India from Madras to Benares by train, he was welcomed by Indian Christians at Nautanwa, a Nepal-border village whose 1,500 people were Muslims, Hindus and Nepalis. The great Himalayan mountain peaks gleamed with eternal snows along the whole northern horizon. Len was "at home" and knew it with all his heart!

After a period of language study, he was appointed to Lohaghat, the doorway into the vast area of jagged mountains, over whose passes came the Tibetan traders each year. Despite fierce loneliness, the next three years were filled to the brim with intense happiness in missionary activity.

Meanwhile, the world was at war. France had fallen and missionaries were being called up. Len travelled to Bangalore and enlisted on August 21st, 1940. He cabled for Iris. Things moved into top gear. By special licence they were married on April 15th, 1941, and within two weeks Len was away to Iraq. Four further years of separation lay ahead of the couple.

In March 1945, Len and Iris enjoyed an all-too-brief sixty-one days of leave, during which they visited some of Len's previous Tibetan friends. What joy all round! "When are you coming back?" was the burning question, as yet unanswerable. But of one thing they were certain: that they would come back.

Len had to return to military duties. Nine months later, he was released from the army. He was full of plans as to how he could reach all the known villages on the Tibetan border. He trekked endlessly, and everywhere shared the gospel with all whom he met.

In May 1947, Len planned one final long trek, before he and Iris would return home for furlough. Leaving the mission base, he would trek up to Mansiari, an outpost of the London Missionary Society many years before, and then on, if possible to Milam, right on the Tibetan border. This was to be a survey trip to plan for future advance. Among the piles of equipment were a cine-camera and enough film to make a record that would challenge all who saw it to pray, and hopefully many to hear God's call to "go and tell".

Len was accompanied by Jac Dyck, a Canadian, who was working with WEC in Nepal. When they reached Mansiari, they were saddened to see the destruction of the old mission buildings, all overgrown by nettles. The two men knelt in the remains and prayed for the future, and for the coming of reinforcements to rebuild that border post. Then they pressed on through one of the greatest gorges of the world to Milam, 12,000 feet above sea level.

Still on and on, climbing up and up, to reach the summit of the 17,000 foot pass, THREE MILES HIGH. Their drovers became snow-blind and quite unable to help or advise them on the route: but they made their goal!

Eventually back to base, and the journey home to England for a much-needed break and rest. On September 8th, 1947, Len and Iris, with their twenty-one-month-old son Noel, arrived back in London. For a rest? Never!

Thirty-five years old, this burning enthusiast never

considered rest to be an essential part of his programme. He had come home to enthuse others with the needs of the Tibetan people. Hadn't he shot reel after reel of film on those arduous treks over the roof of the world? The first three months at home were mainly spent splicing the film together.

At last, *Three Miles High* was ready. Ninety-three meetings were organised, throughout the length and breadth of the United Kingdom. There were camps and conferences and school assemblies. The film was a tremendous success, and young people flocked to talk to Len after the showings. *Three Miles High* challenged right through to the core of a person – how far was one willing to go for Jesus, who had gone all the way to Calvary for us?

1949 – Preparing reinforcements

For some years, WEC staff had felt that God was leading the mission to establish their own missionary training college (MTC).

During the previous two years, God had singularly blessed Francis and Elsie Rowbotham in the Scottish Regional Headquarters. They had built up many contacts with young people and had much blessing in their youth camps. As a result, they began to sense that God was calling *them* to develop this urgently needed training facility.

"The first thing we need to look to the Lord for", Elsie told her husband, "is trained staff, as we ourselves do not have the necessary qualifications. Secondly," she added, almost as an afterthought, "we shall need to extend our premises."

God was also working in the hearts of Stewart and Marie Dinnen. They were actually living in the Scottish headquarters, while completing Bible College training in Glasgow. Stewart had a Master of Arts degree from Glasgow University, plus a teacher's diploma of education. Marie was a trained nurse.

"As we joined the Rowbothams in prayer for God's guidance with regard to the opening of a WEC training centre here in the Glasgow Headquarters," Marie wrote, "we could see the priceless advantage of such a centre where the academic, though by no means disparaged, would not have more than its rightful place in a course that was to be vitally spiritual and practical.

"Suddenly, during one of the all-nights of prayer," she continued, "God challenged us with the fact that He had given *us* experience and background which could prove useful in such a programme . . . but . . ."

But . . . and there seemed to be a thousand "buts".

Eventually, through a talk with Norman Grubb one day, their doubts were put to rest and they *knew* that this was God's plan for their lives. They moved forward to prepare themselves with two periods of in-service training, first to WEC London Headquarters, and then to the Bible College of Wales, at Swansea.

During 1949, planning for the new MTC went on apace, until a declaration of intent to open the College on October 5th, appeared in the magazine. Before this could actually happen, there would have to be the completion of purchase and furnishing of a new extension building. Could it ever be done?

In April 1949, the Rowbothams and Dinnens started praying earnestly that the Lord would provide alternative accommodation for the four families living in the adjoining property to the WEC Glasgow Headquarters. This property should then be put on the market at a price they could afford – and one after another, they watched those four families move out, and saw the house go up for sale!

The owners wanted £4,500. The Rowbothams had £200. Could God? Why not? He had done greater things in the past. "All He demanded was that we believed Him," Elsie stated with great simplicity.

So, in June, they entered into a contract, that the money and keys should be exchanged on September 16th. In July, the Rowbothams received £2,000: in August, the

Dinnens received £1,000, as a seal on their call to this new venture. Then a whole string of small gifts came in. The total crept up to £4,000. "The day arrived," recorded Elsie, "when the house was to be legally ours, but we lacked £500. What could we do? We waited on God, but nothing seemed to happen." September 16th had passed. The 1st of October arrived. The students were due on the 5th.

The Rowbothams went and laid the whole matter before the lawyer.

"Why not take out a mortgage?" the lawyer suggested.

Was the devil tempting them? That was against the mission's principles.

"Could we have the keys for the £4,000, on the promise of early payment of the remaining outstanding £500?" Fran queried.

The lawyer assured them that would be quite out of order and impossible to arrange – "it just isn't done like that!"

However – despite him – the keys arrived two days later, on October 3rd.

On the morning of October 5th the staff stood in the empty house: no beds, no floor coverings. Then followed a string of miracles! A message came from the Irish Steamship Company to say that bedding had arrived at the docks for them to collect. A friend brought some iron bedsteads. Another sent enough linoleum to cover the floors. As the students arrived, they deposited their luggage in the hall, rolled up their sleeves and got on with the job of turning the naked house into their new home. By bedtime, with all floors covered and everyone with a bed to sleep on, staff and students, though extremely tired, were wonderfully happy!

Early on the Tuesday morning, the Lord spoke. "Can you trust Me to give you that £500 this week?" "Yes, Lord." Was this to be the new MTC's first corporate lesson in the school of faith? They had a half-night of prayer. Wednesday they had a day of prayer and fasting. Throughout the whole week, their faith was tested, until the following Tuesday morning a letter from Northern Ireland was received containing a cheque for the needed £500, and the Missionary Training College was a fully-paid-for reality!

1950 – Breaking down barriers

"1950 ADVANCE – INDONESIA ENTERED." So cried the front page of the January magazine, with two announcements – that Harold Williams, with Heini and Agnes Germann-Edey, had entered West Borneo, in fellowship and close collaboration with the Christian and Missionary Alliance team, and that Gladys Rusha had sailed on New Year's Day for the island of Celebes, in collaboration with the Salvation Army, for orientation at their Macassar leprosy camp.

The Borneo trio were tremendously helped and encouraged by their host Mission, as also by the workers of the Borneo Evangelistic Mission. Very soon they had been led to two needy areas three days up river from the coast, among the Dyak people. They had the loan of a motor launch until they could procure their own, and were already digging into language study.

They were out on trek most weeks, in different directions, among totally unreached people, who were living like those of the Stone Age. The poverty and wretchedness was indescribable. The great curse was the locally brewed rice-beer, of an unbelievable potency, destroying the people physically and mentally. Only slightly less fearsome was the chewing of the betel-nut, mixed with lime and tobacco leaves. Their objects for worship were often just a stick of wood, a tree, a rock in the river, or an elusive bird.

Gladys wrote from Celebes of desperately primitive conditions and of extraordinary loneliness. From the time of her arrival, all the other staff had left, and she found herself in charge of the busy dispensary and the leprosy care centre, with practically no knowledge of the local language. She was surrounded by an uncaring, indifferent and fatalistic people, who accepted death as their lot, and who believed that the leprosy patients were already dead.

"They are difficult people, I know," she wrote, "but surely the Lord has some way of reaching through to them and bringing them to Himself. I do pray that I may never get used to men and women living and dying without God."

By the end of the year, Gladys left Celebes and flew to join the other Crusaders in West Borneo, where WEC planned to open their own leprosy care centre. At the same time Margaret Williams arrived from Australia to join her husband, and Olaf Myheim from Britain. As the party of three travelled slowly, tediously, up river, they stopped one evening at a small village, and were shown into a long-house kept for passing travellers. All their equipment was off-loaded, and they were told to wait for another boat to take them further into the interior.

"Mother, Mother, there it is! There it is!"

Tiny feet pattered across the loosely tied slats, and hands grabbed frantically at a woman's scanty black skirt. Indescribable horror filled all their eyes. Children and mother shrank backwards through a doorway into the darkness of the opposite long-house and a tense silence settled, as they waited the reappearance of the white apparition.

"They had peered into our quarters and seen these two insipid-looking beings with yellowish hair and lightish eyes," wrote Gladys, "and our boxes and drums piled around us. Who were we? What had we come for? Conjecture flew in every direction. Dyaks have wild imaginations and someone decided the drums were full of snakes. That was the last straw, and the children buried their heads in their mothers' laps.

"When we attempted to explain that we had come to bring them good news of Someone who loved them and longed to help them, disbelief overwhelmed them. Love? What was that? No one asks for love; no one ever sees the need to give it. All live for themselves, in callous selfishness. Our love of giving and serving them only builds a higher wall of suspicion. They cannot understand. They have never met anyone who cared."

"Can we sing to you?" asked Margaret. "We sang,

talked and prayed: to them it was just the white man's witchcraft. Dear Lord, where do we start?"

Yet, within the year, barriers were being broken down and many were beginning to listen to the gospel. Australian nurse Isabel Stephenson had joined the group, and was working eighteen hours a day in the medical outreach work. Gladys was establishing the leprosy care centre. Agnes Germann-Edey wrote of the exciting school work. "We have had the joy of opening a school here, with twenty-eight Dyak and Chinese boys and girls. You should have seen the children arriving in their canoes, from ten different villages, scattered far and near in the jungle. Many of them had never seen a white-skinned person before. We have managed to build a schoolroom with the help of some of the local folk. It is wonderful to hear them learning gospel hymns morning and evening, before and after classes."

1951 – Modern-day Inquisition

"On a summer's night in 1951," recalled Willie Easton, "three young Colombians and I were chosen by the Lord to suffer in Mariquita for His Name's sake. There were only eight of us at the meeting that night – two teenage girls, my wife and six-year-old son Lawrence, myself, twenty-three-year-old Saul, twenty-two-year-old Gonzalo and nineteen-year-old Jorge. We were halfway through the meeting, when a sergeant and three policemen arrived. The sergeant strode straight up to Gonzalo, standing in the pulpit, Bible in hand.

"'What book is that?'

"'The Bible.'

"I called out that I was the pastor, to draw his attention away from Gonzalo.

"Just then, the Inspector of Police arrived, with a plain-clothes detective. The sergeant handed over the Bibles and a hymn book, declaring they were bad books and should be burned.

"'One of those is my personal property,' I remonstrated, 'You have no right to burn it!'

"That was all they were waiting for. The man stepped back, measured his distance, and dealt me two terrific blows with the flat of his sabre. Little Lawrence screamed. The women and girls were ordered out, with the child.

"One of the men leapt forward, dealing me a blow on the forehead with the butt of his rifle. It sent me reeling backwards. No sooner had I regained my balance, than he clubbed me again. I went down. Dazed, and wiping the blood from my face, I saw Gonzalo and Jorge lying on their backs, trying to ward off as many blows as possible. We were ordered to lie on the ground, and they savagely kicked us, jumped on us and beat us with the butt-end of their guns.

"Marched off down the main street, denounced as communists, we were shoved into the back-yard of the notorious police barracks. They made us trot round and round the yard, while they struck us as we passed them. Given heavy sticks, we had to beat each other, and any sign of leniency was rewarded with further brutality from the police. Lain flat on our stomachs, we were forced to drag ourselves across the yard by clutching small tufts of grass, a most painful and tiring ordeal.

"We were forced to drink from a filthy drain. Whilst stretched out full length on the ground, a policeman put his foot on the backs of our necks and pressed our faces deep in the muck.

"They called me out to make me sing to them, and then one of them put his foot behind me, and with his fist knocked me to the ground. Over and over again. It all went on and on.

"The Inspector arrived with the three Bibles. He interrogated me about them, and I seized the opportunity to tell them of the love of God and of salvation in Jesus. Infuriated, he put a bottle of petrol in my hand, and forced me to burn the books, standing over me with a raised stick.

"The boys behaved magnificently throughout. No

protest, complaint or plea for mercy escaped their lips. Nothing was too vile for the police in their humiliation of us. Unmentionable things . . . they left me with the feeling that the citadel of one's soul was forever stained.

"Suddenly all but one left. He ordered us to strip while he went for his rifle. I committed myself and the boys to the Lord, sensing this was the end. Returning, he ordered us into an adjoining yard of a rice-threshing mill, filled with great dunes of burning chaff. He stood us in a line on the top, in the moonlight. Surely he would shoot us now. The silence and suspense were awful.

"Instead, he ordered us to roll in the chaff, and our lacerated bodies smarted with the heat. Ordered back to the first yard, we had to drag ourselves around as before, lying on our stomachs, without bending our knees. It was excruciating. He forced us to approach the smouldering Bibles, with our faces close to the ashes, blowing them into flames, filling each other's face with smoke and embers. Grimy and with smarting eyes, he ordered us to get dressed, and then to plunge again into the tank of filthy water.

"Led into the barracks lobby, we shivered in our wet clothes. The sergeant returned and ordered us to leave.

"'Don't go, Don Guillermo,' Saul shouted to me. 'Even if you walk, he will provoke you to run and shoot you under the pretence that you tried to escape!'

"Furious at Saul's brave exhortation and outspoken condemnation, he beat him about the shins to make him get down on his knees, but he would not. We held our breath, silently watching his sufferings.

"As the hands of the clock crawled close to midnight, they demanded that I preach them a sermon 'to pass the time of day'. So I told them of the love of God, of the sinfulness of man, and of salvation from sin. But I was not allowed to continue.

"'Do you love this man?' they demanded of each of the boys in turn. Saul courageously and defiantly answered them: 'Yes, I love him and his doctrines!' They buffeted him and punched him in the face, but he never bowed his head to them. They lashed us over the shoulders and around the neck with their studded leather belts, before marching us away to the municipal jail.

"Next day, they paraded us through town, to the mayor's office. 'I've decided to let you go free,' the Mayor stated magnanimously, 'on condition you do not report the affair to higher authorities' – and so God released us from this modern-day inquisition."

1952 – Middle-aged – still spreading?

Almost forty years old – time to look back, look around and look forward. What had the mission achieved in these first forty years? What were they at present planning? What was their long-term objective?

From the outset, the goal had been to reach all the remaining unreached people of the world with the good news of the gospel of Jesus Christ, in the shortest possible time. From the tiny start at Niangara in the north-eastern corner of the Belgian Congo (Zaïre), evangelisation teams had spread rapidly over the length and breadth of the four provinces in the area, until almost every tribal group had come under the sound of the gospel.

Then the work had spread to South America, via Brazil to Colombia: along the West Coast of Africa, from Senegal, via Portuguese Guinea (Guinea Bissau), Liberia, Ivory Coast, Gold Coast (Ghana) and on to Spanish Guinea (Equatorial Guinea): to India and Kashmir, to the Tibetan and Nepalese borders: and so through to Indonesia. Work was carried on amongst the outcastes and tribal peoples, amongst city dwellers and university students, through preaching, teaching and medical care.

Home bases were operating vigorously in the United Kingdom, Canada, the United States, Australia, New Zealand and Holland, and most recently, Germany; with several regional headquarters and numerous prayer support groups all over each of these countries. A missionary training college had been opened, to prepare candidates for the rigours of the task ahead, both in spiritual and practical ways. A home had been opened for the care of the children of the missionaries.

The Christian Literature Crusade had been born from the parent Crusade. In Zaïre, the Leper and Medical Crusade had struggled to birth, and was now operating in seven different countries.

In 1945, at the end of World War Two, a survey of remaining "black spots" had drawn attention to the specific need of twenty-seven areas where no missionary work was as yet being carried on. Steadily, these were being entered: in 1946, the Canary Isles; 1947, Siam (Thailand) alongside the Christian and Missionary Alliance; 1948, China, alongside the China Inland Mission and many others; 1949, Chinese-Tibet; 1950, Japan, alongside the Japan Evangelistic Band; Pakistan, alongside the Bible and Medical Missionary Fellowship, and Indonesia; and in 1951, Uruguay. Some of the records of penetration into these eight previously "black" areas were filled with marvellous stories of God's gracious provision and protection.

Mr and Mrs Cooper, soon to be followed by Margaret Phillips and Violet Edson, sailed for Tenerife in 1946 to take up again missionary labours that they had commenced many years before.

"Bangkok at last!" wrote Wilf and Evy Overgaard, October 23rd, 1947, as he and his wife settled in for a year's language study before going up into the interior to a region as yet unentered by any other missionary group.

"Margaret Landahl has had the joy of leading her Chinese language teacher and his wife to the Lord," wrote David Woodward in 1948 from the China Tibetan border; telling of many who were finding the Saviour, Chinese and Tibetan.

In 1949, Edith Seager, in Tibet, wrote of riding horseback for eighteen days through the indescribable beauty of the mountains between Kanting and Kantze, as they (three single women) made their way with a cavalcade of yak!

Following Ken Adams' expeditionary trip to Japan, WEC and CLC had asked God for ten workers for Japan before the end of 1950. The Nicholsons and Fultons from USA and Ray Oram from UK all sailed before November 1950, and seven others had been accepted and were preparing to leave!

Margaret Brown and Lily Boal wrote of the sheer thrill of unpacking their bags in Pakistan. Jim Finlay returned to Uruguay, where he had taught in schools eighteen years before, and now came as a missionary to the land of his adoption.

"And what more shall I say? Time (and space) would fail me to tell of . . ."

Ahead, there were still an alarming number of areas totally unreached by any mission agency, with millions of people completely outside the sound of the gospel. The challenge "to reach all the remaining unreached people in the shortest possible time" had not changed. The declaration still stood that "If Jesus Christ be God and died for me, then no sacrifice can be too great for me to make for Him." Only the supreme sacrifice by every member of the team could enable the task to be achieved before the end of the century. Only by simple faith in God could the job be done. But with these, the mission could look forward, seeing the impossibilities of the challenge, and knowing that "in Him all things are possible."

Yet at the same time, from all the fields, there rose an urgent cry of the need for revival. A great discontent filled the hearts of many of the 460 missionaries and of multitudes of national pastors on every field, and importunate prayer was being made everywhere that God would do a new work in their midst, pouring out His Holy Spirit to cleanse and purify His Church.

Part Three

HOLINESS

1953–1968

"It is about time we put on the brakes," Len Moules challenged the WEC family at the close of the 1950s. "Christianity is being challenged, and we are becoming the pacemakers in this colossal race. We are so heavily committed and intense in our methods, that we are in danger of substituting these for our real objective, which is to reveal the *holiness* of God to the praise of His glory.

"God's power and purposes are through personnel. And what repulsive material we are (Eph. 2:1–3), what human debris! But to God's glory, through the atonement, we are completely rehabilitated by divine love and sacrifice; we are forgiven prodigals; we are sons of God.

"Let mission executives and Christian leaders beware that we do not emphasise the stature (academic qualifications) of a man in enrolling our missionary recruits. God emphasises holy living in love. He underlines the characteristic of likeness to Himself. God wants them to be to the praise of His glory. These are His unchanging standards. Academic knowledge and the skill of the professions find their service only accepted and blessed by divine hands when there is a heart also that is holy.

"God seeks to reveal His holiness. He plans to destroy sin. He purposes to create holy people. God calls us to live holy lives. It is not necessarily more activity – but of necessity more holiness. It is not to throw great resources of equipment into Christian warfare, but to bring into the battle hearts pure and aflame with the indwelling Saviour.

"Let us cease to be pacemakers for God, but men at peace with God."

"Thou Christ of burning cleansing flame"

Thou Christ of burning cleansing flame, Send the Fire!
Thy Blood-bought gift today we claim, Send the Fire!
    Look down and see this waiting host;
    Give us the promised Holy Ghost,
    We want another Pentecost;
       Send the Fire!

God of Elijah, hear our cry; Send the Fire!
Twill make us fit to live or die: Send the Fire!
    To burn up every trace of sin,
    To bring the light and glory in;
    The revolution now begin,
       Send the Fire!

Tis Fire we want, for Fire we plead, Send the Fire!
The Fire will meet our every need; Send the Fire!
    For strength to ever do the right,
    For grace to conquer in the fight,
    For power to walk the world in white,
       Send the Fire!

To make our weak hearts strong and brave, Send the
  Fire!
To live a dying world to save, Send the Fire!
    Oh, see us on Thy altar lay
    Our lives, our all, this very day;
    To crown the offering now we pray,
       Send the Fire!

1953 – Aflame for God

During April and May 1953, Jessie Scholes had been very ill with black-water fever. In June, she went with Jack for a few weeks of convalescence, first to Bomili and then further south to Opienge.

"As we came into the village", the leader of the Congo team wrote later, "we knew at once, by the singing and the joy on all their faces, that God had done a new thing."

On returning from Opienge, the Scholes went to the regular Friday evening testimony meeting in the Ibambi Bible School. Jack had just begun to share a little of what he had seen and heard to the south, when "the Holy Spirit came down in mighty power.

"There was a growing sound outside, as of a gathering storm. Yet the palm-trees stood erect, silhouetted against the calm night sky. Suddenly the very building was shaken! We know something now of what it must have been like at the Day of Pentecost. As one prayed, then another, then the whole congregation together – such a noise as they poured out their hearts, some in desperate confession of sin, others in overwhelming praise to God. Men, women, boys and girls, were 'drunk' with the Spirit, many shaking beyond their control, some throwing themselves to the ground in grief and under strong conviction, others standing with upraised arms, worshipping and singing. We stood amazed and at first fearful. But God gave us the assurance that this was Himself at work in our midst. If it had not been of God it would have been terrible, as they were beyond human control."

From all areas, letters began to stream into Ibambi telling of similar mighty outpourings of the Spirit. "Words cannot tell . . ." "We have never seen anything like it before . . ." "Words fail to describe . . ." and so on, wrote the awed missionaries.

Some wrote of reaping in days what had been sown through many years. All spoke of marvellously changed lives and that "those who stole, steal no more." Every missionary asked for prayer that they might be enabled to deal with those under conviction of sin, listening almost constantly to folk confessing without becoming numbed or immune. There was the need of godly wisdom in dealing with the fanatical ones. "We had one friend dashing into our house early in the morning with a 'message' that 'all the stars have names and so have all the people!' He wanted to dash off to the official's house to ask him if his name was written in the Lamb's Book of Life, and if not, to tell him he was on the road to hell . . . We had to point out that the Spirit respects law and order. We think a better way to reach the expatriates, is as Dawidi did. He went to ask the Greek shopkeeper to forgive him for wrongfully obtaining paraffin, and saying he would return the stolen oil as soon as he could. Another, Bir Ali, stole an axe and a spade when in prison some years ago. Now he is awaiting the official's return to give them back to him. The Belgians and Cypriots are all amazed!"

"Beauty for ashes . . ." "Glorious and wonderful . . ." "Great is the glow . . .", so the letters continued to report from every corner of the Congo work.

"Conviction of sin just tears us down, when He is at work in our hearts," wrote the missionary in charge at Wamba. "Even schoolboys are on their feet, pleading for mercy as they see their sins as sinful." The letter continued with a description of the weekly evening of prayer when folk began to crowd into the church, and others stood all around outside. "The meeting was simple. One catechist began to tell about the way God was working at his village. Then a woman started to give her testimony. I am not clear as to whether she finished or not, because the power of the Spirit fell upon the assembly. There was a spontaneous outbreak of prayer, many people taking part, while some cried in agony of soul for mercy and pardon. As I sat there," the missionary recalled, "bewildered and shaken by the turn things had taken, I heard a sound amidst the din, like the sighing of a breeze. This gained strength, until it became a noise such as that that heralds the breaking of a tropical storm."

"I don't think one could exaggerate the degree of Holy Spirit blessing!" wrote Frank Cripps a few weeks later, from Ibambi. "We went to visit a village, and the fire fell. At the camp for the care of the leprosy patients also, the Spirit is working with mighty conviction. Souls are crying out at the awfulness of their sin and finding the Saviour!"

At places hundreds of miles apart, the pattern was the same. Firstly, there came deep conviction of sin and a desperate need to confess all and make restitution wherever possible. Then, to those who had got right with God, and to those who had been praying and believing for revival, there came a fulness of joy that they were honestly unable to contain. They would stand with radiant faces pouring out their hearts in songs of worship for hours on end. New songs were being written from full hearts, always praising for the blood and for all that Jesus had done for them at Calvary. Then there came an almost unbearable burden of prayer for those around who were still unsaved, followed by an urgent need to go out and witness to them. Teams of witness took the gospel to surrounding villages in aggressive evangelism, in a way never before seen. They needed no prompting. Some would set out at 5 a.m. in order to be back in time for 8 a.m. work duties. And hundreds of villagers came to know the Saviour in the ensuing months.

"The hearts of thousands are aflame for God," wrote Jessie, "and dry grounds are being turned into water springs on all sides!"

1954 – The wind blows

South America: "First impressions are most attractive", wrote Jim Finlay from Uruguay; "imposing buildings and magnificent parks, plenty of space and relatively few people, cattle to graze and foreigners to cope with marketing their produce. The rich Uruguayans appear to laugh their way through life.

"But behind all the apparent prosperity and gaiety, Uruguay hides terrible social and spiritual needs. The average wage is insufficient to cover a family's needs, even if kept from gambling and drink. Marriage is more costly than casual unions. The State is atheistic, and no religion can be taught in schools. Gross materialism reigns on all sides, and there is an apathetic indifference to all spiritual need.

"Yet the wind of the Spirit is blowing, and there is a wide open door for evangelism."

Africa: "She has many sides," wrote Leona Pasmore from Spanish Guinea. "There is *suffering* Africa. In one village, I visited the chief's uncle who was very ill. A year ago, he had been a big strapping man, caring neither for his soul nor the gospel. Now he is lying, waiting for death, paralysed from his waist down and unable to speak. We told him once again the way of salvation but we doubt if he could understand.

"There is *heartless* Africa, as the weak, the old and the ailing are left to die alone. I saw a very old woman, lying on a pole bed waiting for death. Deaf, almost blind, skin and bones, a little food is put at her side for her to fumble for. And at the end of her misery, death and eternity await her.

"Then there is *beautiful* Africa. Orchids . . . butterflies . . . birds . . . but as we stand drinking in the loveliness the throbbing of drums reminds us of the curse of witchcraft, and we realise once more that we are in *sinful* Africa; and oh, how we pray for the wind of the Spirit to blow in these parts too."

Siam: "Land of the Free!" William and Rosemary

Charters sent a graphic survey of the land and her peoples. "A land with an abundance of rice, teakwood and tin, exported to eager customers to east and west, and therefore economically sound and with little of the desperate poverty of the rest of the far east.

"Buddhism is the religion of everyone," the missionaries went on to explain; "an attempt by natural man to build a moral system. It includes much that is good, almost equivalent to the Mosaic Law, but God is left out and idols allowed in. One gains merit for one's next life by doing good during this life, such as by feeding the priests or helping with temple buildings. The thought of being punished in a later incarnation for the sins committed in this one, when one cannot remember the previous incarnation, is hardly an incentive to holy living!

"Communism and Christianity are the two intruders, and neither is welcomed. Yet souls are being saved. We have not seen, however, the separation from idolatry and worldliness in these young converts that we long for. May the wind of the Spirit blow through our small congregations, to give us a people genuinely regenerated and living out and out lives for the Lord Jesus Christ."

Jack Masson sent a heart cry from *Japan*: "It was Sunday, and my heart was burdened for the evening service. I made my way to a favourite spot in a local park, where, undisturbed, I could look down over our valley and meditate on their needs. How peaceful it all looks, yet within its heart there is no peace. As far as the eye can see, there are countless hamlets and homes, dominated by the inevitable shrines and temples, 'seats of Satan,' spreading their evil influence of deep darkness.

"How shall we ever reach these people for Christ?" Jack's heart cried out. "Doubtless, only on our knees. Pray for me. I feel our little church in Gokasho is all too weak. I have heard it said that a church is only as strong as its pastor. I would not doubt this, and therefore ask you to pray for me!

"Last Saturday night I went to a meeting, held, by

mistake, in a Buddhist temple. All the Buddhist believers had been primed, and were clutching their ritualistic beads as a means of protection against the message of God's love. Hard faces, stony hearts, and minds already made up to reject all that was offered – yet God's Word is powerful, and the Spirit will blow where He will, and they cannot resist Him for ever."

1955 – The masked face of the devil

"The prayer flags are gaudily waving," wrote Hester Withey, from the Indo-Tibetan border. "They have been recently unfurled in honour of the coming New Year festivities. Familiar and home-like they look, excitedly so, to the locals. But they are not really gay, for they speak again of *the masked face of the devil*, hiding behind the Buddhist front, blinding, binding and damning souls."

Hester had only recently arrived at this northern outpost of the Indian sub-continent, having been evacuated from the eastern border of Tibet in inland China, during the communist take-over of that great land.

One thing the poor beggars of the western border had in common with the swaggering eastern Tibetans was their desperate need to know the gospel. Their friendliness reached only to the point where the missionary began to tell them of the love of the Lord Jesus. Then a barrier was raised. Fear, suspicion, a love of their own ways and hard opposition to anything like change seemed to raise an iron wall of resistance. Yet so many had never before heard of the love of God. One could occasionally see a flicker of curiosity, even a vague hunger, to be allowed to listen further.

"One little family is of deep interest," wrote Hester. "The father, who can read, is away mumbling the Scriptures that we gave him, to other families, to earn a bit of cash. The little mother and her gang of children are busy mending their ragged clothes and shoes, and picking livestock out of each other's hair. There is a little girl of twelve, apparently dying, and they are deeply worried for her in a fatalistic way. They have heard that these 'preachers of religion' have good medicine, with great power – could they heal the girl? She is a pathetic mite, emaciated and jaundiced, with big hollow eyes and swollen face and feet. Around her neck hangs the lama-given charm necklace."

"These foreign people said that their Saviour Jesus could heal our little girl but that no one else could," mused the mother. They had prayed for her daughter, but their prayer was not the "vacant hum" of the priests. It seemed that they talked to Someone whom they could not see, with their eyes shut. But nothing had happened.

Now they have come again. They are trying to explain that, "Our Saviour Jesus can heal and save, but He cannot hear our prayer while that necklace stays around the child's neck. The Lord Jesus has nothing to do with lama affairs."

With tense, utterly serious, almost awe-stricken face the mother took the proffered scissors and the necklace was removed. Hester told them again of Jesus, and then prayed for the child. The mother looked expectantly at the little girl; and with obvious light and dawning faith in her face, she softly repeated to herself "Saviour Jesus, Saviour Jesus!" that she might not forget His Name.

"A few days passed without any obvious change in Tee-ten-dromo, the sick one," wrote Hester, "and the day came when the family had to start on the long journey to the cold north land. They sent for us again as the patient could not make it beyond the town outskirts. We prayed earnestly in the Name of Jesus for the child's healing.

"While the group waited in silence and possibly with faith as a grain of mustard seed, Tee-ten-dromo said her pain was gone! She said it travelled down from her shoulders and tummy, down, down and out of her body. She walked around, at our suggestion, and still had no pain. She ate a little raw flour with no distress, though she could not manage much – but she had not been able to eat anything at all without pain, for weeks."

As the missionaries prepared to return home, the child relaxed into a peaceful rest. The onlooking family were deeply impressed: and the mother, with that same look of dawning light and joy, kept repeating softly to herself, eyes fixed on the little girl, "Thank you, Saviour Jesus! Thank you, Saviour Jesus!"

"The sequel to this story cannot be written," Hester wrote, "but is hidden in the silences of the mighty Himalayas. Will the family remember and did they understand? Did they believe? Will they tell others? What story is being told under the shadow of the prayer flags amidst the snow mountains of this fast-closed land, held in the grip of communism, and the even tighter grip of the lamaistic priesthood?"

1956 – What will they read?

The vast upsurge of literacy throughout the world and the hunger of the masses for something to read challenged WEC to get more involved in producing the right sort of literature to meet the need. During the early 1950s, Trevor Shaw, working with the Sudan Interior Mission, had pioneered the field by producing first *The Africa Challenge* in Nigeria, for anglophones, and then *Envol* in Ivory Coast, for francophones.

The genius of both magazines was that they were utterly indigenous, writers and artists being Africans. They were brought out in bright modern styles, with articles of current news and interest. They were immediate successes, reaching thousands of new readers, catching the imagination of the non-religious and then pointing them to Christ.

The Shaws were invited to the Congo to produce three similar magazines in their three main trade languages, and Fred Chapman was seconded from WEC to work with Trevor at this task. Then God gave Ken Adams and the CLC the vision of a similar outreach by producing *The*

Caribbean Challenge. Gold Coast began *The New Nation*. Other papers were in process of production for Spanish Latin America and South-East Asia.

In December 1959, God laid a great burden on the hearts of Fred and Lois Chapman, during their furlough from Ivory Coast, to produce a *free* paper in simple French, for those who read the language only with difficulty and who were too poor to be able to afford to buy a glossy magazine. Thus *Bientôt* was born, and Gospel Literature Worldwide (GLW) launched. *Soon, Bientôt's* English counterpart, appeared a few years later, first by Dave Cornell in the USA, and then by John and Nellie Lewis, who caught the same vision for English-speaking peoples around the world. These gospel broadsheets were filled with testimonies of those who had come to know Jesus as their Saviour. The sheets were sent out by groups of keen Christian people from their homes, by personal mail to hundreds of thousands of avid readers all over the world.

Today many different language versions are traversing the world every month with the message of reconciliation. Literally millions of copies have been sent out, and God has faithfully provided all the material needed, as well as the finance for production and dissemination. The resulting correspondence with enquirers and those needing counselling, and with others asking for Bible correspondence courses, has reached phenomenal proportions and shows no signs of diminishing with the passing years.

"Soon Clubs" began to come into being, where someone, who had satisfactorily completed four consecutive Bible correspondence courses, could help and encourage other *Soon* readers. These clubs became the foundation stones of new local churches.

A missionary in Senegal then wrote home of a lad who walked through their village every day with a cassette player blaring away. "Why don't we make use of this means of communication?" So now folk are recording all that is written on a *Soon* sheet on to a cassette, and sending that

out to teachers of English in countries all over the world –
including mainland China!

Missionaries in India and other Muslim lands saw the
possibility of developing Bible correspondence courses,
where mail could get through to people and places that they
themselves could not otherwise reach. The Evangelical
Alliance Mission pioneered this approach, and WEC missionaries soon caught the vision and the enthusiasm. Within a year or so, they had over three thousand Indians
enrolled in a two-year course of Bible studies. Over fifty
letters to enquirers were being written daily. Several came
to a knowledge of sins forgiven and many nominal Christians found the living Saviour. The spark spread from
North India, to the Nepal border work, and then on to
Thailand, Java, Japan and Korea.

Throughout the years, other missionaries became increasingly involved in the long, arduous task of translating
the Bible into hitherto unwritten languages, that all people
might be able to read the Scriptures in their own mother
tongue. Isa Arthur's story is a thrilling one to represent all
those who have given years of labour to this supremely
difficult calling. Though trained as a nurse, she arrived in
Portuguese Guinea in November 1956, in answer to the
field's prayer for a linguist to tackle the Bijagos language,
and her own prayer that God would lead her to the neediest
part of the world. She had already completed her training at
Wycliffe and had studied Portuguese in Portugal on her
way out to West Africa.

She flew to Orango, a beautiful palm-strewn island with
white sandy beaches. Evangelist Augusto Fernandes
helped her to learn the language and reduce it to writing.
Her small mud-and-thatch home was just opposite the
circular house of the Bijagos gods, in which Queen Pampa
had been buried along with her thirty-five young (alive)
maidens. Two withered old witches, caked in palm oil
and wearing grass skirts, in charge of the country's
"gods", were Isa's neighbours and friends. And there
she lived for years, translating the New Testament into a

most complex, grammatically intriguing, semi-Bantu language.

In 1977, after twenty-one years of unremitting labour, the first Bijagos New Testaments arrived in Orango. What a day of triumph! Yet rather than sit back and rejoice, Isa immediately left the island, to settle on the mainland, and tackle the translation of the New Testament into Creole!

1957 – Passing on the torch

During the 1940s and 50s, WEC missionaries in India had been led into close fellowship and co-operation with some of God's Spirit-filled Indian witnesses, and it was thrilling to see them picking up the torch. Brother Bakht Singh was one of the most outstanding of these new national missionaries, whom God was singularly blessing. Not only was he an able Bible teacher and church planter but also a trainer of other national brethren, that they too should become evangelists and pastors.

In 1947, Bakht Singh had had to send one of his deputies, Jordan Kahn, to recuperate at Ghoom, a small Indian town south of Darjeeling, in the foothills of the majestic Himalayas, near to the Nepal border.

The fiery spirit within the weak body could not accept respite from the spiritual battle. "It was in September 1947," wrote Brother Jordan Kahn, in a report given ten years later, "when I was sent to Darjeeling, that the Lord sent a spiritual awakening. Many nominal Christians, Hindus and Buddhists were brought under deep conviction of sin and were found openly weeping and repenting. Many were regenerated and the Lord raised a living Church, first in Darjeeling, then in Kalimpong.

"Since 1947 the Spirit of God has been mightily working," Jordan Kahn continued in his report. "All over Kalimpong and Darjeeling districts, groups and assemblies of true believers, Nepalis and Lepchas, have sprung up."

The work grew so rapidly, and spawned so many new

baby-fellowships, that Brother Jordan Kahn cried out: "What can I do? It is an impossible situation. I cannot be in every place at once, yet all these converts need teaching!"

Then a missionary fervour came upon the groups. "From 1949 to 1955," Jordan Kahn explained, "we had been praying that the Lord would remove all hindrances and obstacles and lead us into Nepal to preach the gospel. Then in 1956, when I was praying, the Lord spoke to me very clearly.

"'Go ye into Nepal to preach the gospel.'

"I shared the burden with other brothers, and the Lord confirmed His Word to all our hearts. Though we knew that the preaching of the gospel was forbidden in Nepal, yet we knew that God had commanded us to go, and the Word came to us: 'We ought to obey God rather than man.' I told my fellow-workers that we must be prepared for any sufferings, persecution, opposition, jail or even death. The Lord strengthened us, and we determined to preach the gospel openly and publicly in Nepal at any cost."

So an evangelistic team of four brothers and four sisters was sent towards Nepal. "We marched in," recalled Brother Kahn. "At the border, the Lord wonderfully opened the door for us and we came right into Nepal! As we reached Pashupatti, we all knelt on the ground and prayed. As we finished our prayers, we were amazed to find ourselves surrounded by a crowd of Nepalis. In the Lord's strength I started to preach the gospel in Hindustani at the top of my voice. Brother Fudong interpreted into Nepali. It was market day and a huge crowd gathered. All of them stood quietly, saying: 'It is *good*!'"

The Indian evangelists continued from place to place in the market, talking with groups and individuals, men and women. "When the police heard, they rushed to us and told us that it was forbidden to preach there: but the people were listening intently . . . what could they do? Nothing!"

Thousands of tracts, booklets and gospels were sold and distributed. The team returned to Darjeeling, and gave their reports like Paul and Barnabas in olden days. "It stirred up many saints to pray with a deeper burden than ever before, claiming Nepal for Christ." Two more "invasions" were made to Pashupatti and a few surrounding villages. Then the burden of prayer increased that they might reach Kathmandu, the very capital of Nepal, and there also "preach the gospel with all boldness."

"The Lord gave us the promise of Isaiah 54:2, 3, and of Revelation 3:7, 8; 'Behold, I have set before thee an open door and no man can shut it!'" And so a team of eight brothers and sisters marched towards Kathmandu. On the way, they were arrested and taken before the magistrate. Explaining that all they were doing was preaching the gospel of the Lord Jesus Christ, he allowed them to go! "It is indeed wonderful to know that 'Our God reigneth!' He can indeed stop the mouths of lions and open the gates of iron," the team exclaimed.

Eventually, in 1957, they reached the great city of Kathmandu. After a night of prayer, they distributed tracts all over the centre of the town. Then they went from street corner to street corner, singing and preaching the good news. Crowds gathered everywhere, and heard with amazement and interest. Some openly confessed their sins and accepted the Lord Jesus as their personal Lord and Saviour. After three weeks of intensive evangelism, the team returned to India.

A group of Kalimpong Christians were then chosen to go and reside in Kathmandu and establish a focal point of fellowship for the new converts, to strengthen, teach and encourage them. At the same time, other groups were moving into Sikkim and Bhutan. It was the start of a new era, of intense evangelism by nationals, rather than by foreigners.

1958 – Out beyond Trail's End

Since 1929, Mr and Mrs Gordon Smith had worked as independent pioneer missionaries in Cambodia and South

Vietnam. Now they were increasingly burdened to reach out to the vast untouched regions in central Vietnam.

They would have gone to these tribes before, had the Japanese and French wars not intervened. The cease-fire in 1954 freed the missionaries to re-enter the land, south of the seventeenth parallel. The area was inhabited by primitive, semi-savage mountain peoples, with no written languages, no schools, no medical service.

After a year of language study and adaptation, Mrs Smith describes their eventual arrival, in 1958, among the Cua people. "As we progressed inland," she recalled, "steep rocky hills came down to the road. Then we reached Trail's End, the Vietnamese village of Tra Bong. This was the last settlement of the yellow men, before going into the land of the brown-skinned tribespeople. The great mountains of jungle wilderness that houses the 20,000 Cua people spread like a horseshoe around the village."

That first evening they spoke to the villagers in the market place, with the help of Anh Hai, a Vietnamese interpreter. Everyone seemed curious and interested. The next day they were joined by crowds of Cua tribesfolk coming to market with their bundles of green tea-leaves and cinnamon bark.

The paramount chief of the tribe met the Smiths and invited them to his village of six long-houses, built on stilts, each with a row of dark smoky rooms opening on to a front verandah and approached up a notched pole-ladder. Alcohol jars stood by each doorway: spears and crossbows were stuck in the thatched roof. Dried meat hung in evil-smelling bundles over the open mud fire-boxes. Pigs and chickens dug in the muck underneath the houses. Looking out over the deep valley one could see the foaming river far below and towering mountains on all sides.

"We'll never forget our meeting that night in this Cua village," the Smiths recorded. "We showed flannelgraphs for an hour or so and the tribal audience was spellbound. To our great joy, the chief's son, Long, and his wife, Huong, came forward to commit their lives to the Saviour.

Another, Quang, asked us to visit his village across the river, and to share with his people 'these good words'."

They went with him, the next day, to a huddled group of blackened bamboo houses, amidst muddy rice patches. Inside, the houses were encrusted with soot, cobwebs and dirt. Quang's brother, the big chief on that side of the river, welcomed them kindly. After a tribal dance to the rhythm of the gongs, the chief called for silence, so that they could listen to the "foreigners' message".

Anh Hai again translated the missionaries' French into Vietnamese, and Quang in turn interpreted into Cua. Never before had these people heard the gospel. After the story of creation and man's sin, they heard of the coming of Christ as the world's Redeemer. Flannelgraph was used to depict the crucifixion, resurrection and ascension. It was all like a glimpse of wonderland to those simple mountain people. Practically the whole group asked how they could become Christians. It seemed as though they had just been waiting for someone to come: they accepted the message so simply and easily. God had truly prepared their hearts.

In a month or so, the Smiths moved on to the Hrey tribe, with five new Cua believers going with them, to share testimony to their new-found faith in Christ.

As they reached the Son Ha River valley, they were brought to a standstill, first by the breathtaking view before them, but then by the realisation that here was another large tribe who had never yet heard the gospel. Scores of Hrey villages were dotted throughout the groves of graceful areca-nut palms. Ninety-thousand people were suddenly within their reach. The chief, clad only in loin cloth and necklaces of beads, grinned at the missionaries through the stumps of his teeth, red from the betel-nut juice.

To the chanting of a young sorcerer, seeking to appease the demons who had brought sickness to a young child, the missionary group told the wonderful good news, and that no demons can exist where Jesus is worshipped.

Then followed a big sacrifice of a water buffalo, with dancing and drinking throughout the night. The cruelty and savagery were terrible to behold. The missionaries were sickened by the whole frenzied scene, the gongs and tom-toms never ceasing their monotonous beat. When morning came, they seized the opportunity to tell of the sacrifice of the great Son of God – and God wrought a miracle! In the midst of all the evil, two young Hrey tribesmen believed, simply and joyously accepting that great sacrifice on Calvary's Cross on their behalf.

So the work in central Vietnam began. The first seven students from the tribes gathered together in Da Nang to study the Word of God, before returning as evangelists to their own people. The gospel had begun to penetrate yet one more of Satan's strongholds.

1959 – A horse-happy kid

"Meet Joan Eley. Killing snakes, counselling converts, concreting floors, climbing tortuous tracks, crossing flooded creeks; cracking fierce dogs on the head, catering for youth camps, carrying out her own plumbing and vehicle repairs, caring for sick fellow-worker Dorcas – you can't but gasp at this girl's versatility and vivaciousness, as she tells her humour-laden story of pioneer work for Christ in a semi-desert region of Venezuela." So reads the publisher's blurb on an Australian missionary's autobiography.

"August 1st, 1947. Dad suggests that I be a jillaroo for him," Joan had written in her diary as a fifteen year old. "Work five and a quarter days per week: responsible for tractor driving, bringing in the cows, clearing cultivation paddocks, burning off, driving truck, cutting burr, doing fencing, mustering the sheep and being a general rouse-about in the shearing shed."

So Joan had left school, having had barely three years of formal education, to start the work which did more to train her for her future pioneer life in South America than anything else could possibly have done.

Joan knew that though she might be "a horse-happy kid", she was also disillusioned, with a great void in her heart, "living one hundred per cent for myself." She knew she was making a mess of her life, and tearing her home apart. Several times she contemplated suicide, but her mother always caught her in time. While publicly ridiculing everything that had to do with Christianity, on hearing a fiery sermon at a Christian Endeavour tea, she wrote: "I trembled and shook as I thought of my life. When Mr Smith invited us to accept Jesus into our hearts, so that He could save us from our sins and from hell, I did."

From then on, Joan grew apace in spiritual things. In September 1952, "The 'ye' in 'Go ye into all the world' became '*me*'!" She became a passionate and ardent soul-winner, revelling in the joy and privilege of sharing Jesus with others. Two years later, she met up with WEC. At a convention meeting, Len Moules talked of his work on the Tibetan border. Later, she heard the testimonies of Gerhard and Audrey Bargen, both of whom had been through Japanese prisoner-of-war camps, being captured on their way to India as young WEC missionary candidates. For Joan, that sealed her call to the missionary family of WEC.

Bible College was a nightmare challenge to her who had had so little previous experience of formal education, but God honoured her stickability and gave her success in her exams.

"January 25th, 1959. I have been finally accepted into WEC!"

Sensing a call to Japan, the problem of language learning not only proved an impossibility, but also helped to redirect her thinking from Japan to the country where the Lord actually wanted her – Venezuela.

"November 25th, 1959. Finally arrived in the land of my adoption!"

The initial shock of loneliness and the frustration of not being able to communicate were hard to endure. Every time she walked through a village square, "All I could do was to stand there dumbly not saying a word, yet my heart just longing to tell them about Jesus.

"The Lord's place for me at this time is language study," she came to realise, "so I must take this craving to share the gospel to the Cross. One day the Lord will bring resurrection life out of this death."

And indeed He did! During 1960, Joan joined forces with a wonderful national Christian lady. Hilda, despite a terribly hard upbringing of great suffering, had come to a knowledge of sins forgiven just four years previously through the preaching of Wilf Watson, an itinerant WEC missionary, working then in Venezuela. On January 1st, 1961, the two of them started work together in one of the most primitive areas imaginable, "civilisation left behind!" They were amongst a country people in a semi-desert area called Guadi with its neighbouring tiny villages of El Habra and San Mateo, not even mentioned on Venezuelan maps. Hot, with no electricity or refrigerators or running water, Joan saw this as being "just up my alley!" There were tiny churches there, but no pastor, and no one teaching the handful of believers about the deeper Christian life.

One year after their arrival, "One of our brethren is making more forms for the church," Joan's diary recorded. Why? "The place is packed . . . they come from near and far, young and old, saved and unsaved, educated and uneducated. They are all making their way to the house of God with hungry hearts."

1960 – Called to launch out once again

For a number of years, Fran and Elsie Rowbotham had organised summer holiday conferences for young and old, in different beauty spots of Scotland. These had become very popular, so much so that the Rows (as they have been known for years) began to wonder if God was calling them to develop a conference *centre*, as part of the WEC outreach ministry.

In December 1959, someone drew their attention to a house and estate at Kilcreggan, only thirty-one miles from Glasgow. It was beautifully situated, but the owner wanted £6,000 for it. As they had not a penny, they put it out of their minds.

In January 1960, a phone call from the WEC headquarters in London asked Fran what he thought of the Kilcreggan property. The answer was clear: "We cannot consider it, although in some respects it is just what we need." A week later, the same caller rang: "Would you accept the property as a gift?" Fran could hardly believe his ears! "Yes: I'd take it with both hands!" he almost cried into the phone.

Both the Rows were already deeply involved with other commitments, not least as house parents at the Missionary Training College in Glasgow. What is more, neither had had a proper holiday for two years. Could they really take on this new project?

With clear assurance from God's Word that this was of Him, they moved ahead.

"Could you be ready for conferences this summer?" came a request from headquarters. They began rapid calculations, and said a daring "Yes!"

The house as it was could accommodate only sixty guests: they would therefore need twelve new wooden chalets. A friend in Ireland promised, at his own expense, to send two workmen for six weeks to do the building. All the necessary materials were prayed in; and a few days before the first conference was due to start, the chalets were completed – by a veritable army of volunteers.

One mile of sheeting was made up into bed linen by a team of willing ladies. Drains were laid by a volunteer plumber. One hundred bedsteads and mattresses, 250 blankets, one hundred pillows, pillowslips and bed covers, cooking stove, water heaters . . . all were miraculously provided.

Financial gifts, big and small, helped meet all the recurring bills, until one day they were faced with an outstanding statement for £2,000. They prayed that this might be speedily cleared.

God said clearly: "Your prayer is answered."

"Thank you, Lord," replied Elsie.

The next morning a letter arrived from the Manager of the Bank of Scotland: "A draft for £2,042 to be used for Kilcreggan House – client wishes to remain anonymous."

But what about staff to run the centre? The Rows thought of Margaret Barron, recently widowed. They wrote, telling her of the home and of their need for a house mother. Within a few days, Margaret joined them, sure that this was God's appointment for her at that time. So many have been blessed by her happy and vivacious spirit that never wilted in the ensuing years, despite all the trials and difficulties. Gaye Nicholson, recently graduated from the Glasgow MTC, joined the team and was Margaret's faithful helper for many years.

The next problem that faced the Rows was the care of the five acres of land. They were told of a student at the Bible College who had fifteen years' experience as a gardener – would he be the one of the Lord's choice? Yes! and what a transformation he worked in the grounds.

At the close of 1960, the Rows received a huge gift of £11,000 on the death of a dear friend, and this enabled them to put up and equip another row of chalets during 1961, before the next conference season started.

Year after year, as a direct result of the eight weeks of summer conferences, many have been saved, others called into training for full-time missionary service, some challenged to open their homes to start prayer cells, and yet others to give of their substance to support missionaries in a way they had never considered previously.

1961 – Slim fingers

"I have often listened to your Bible Quiz programme," wrote a child of eight from the Caribbean to the home of

Radio Worldwide, "and here is the answer to this week's question. I hope it is right and that you will send me a copy of the New Testament as my prize. And I do want to be a Christian, so will you please tell me how to be saved?"

What is the story behind such an amazing remark? Who and what is Radio Worldwide, and how did it come into being?

"Eighty every minute. Roughly forty-four million every year," reported Phil Booth, in August 1960, to WEC staff. "Before I finish this report, 300 more. More what? People alive in this world than when I started."

Christians are responsible to reach these "forty-four million more people every year" with the gospel. Phil had done some research, and found that all the dedicated sacrificial living and giving of missionary forces worldwide was reaching an estimated four million extra people a year. "What happens to the other forty million?" he had asked himself.

"Is God abandoning them without an opportunity of ever hearing the gospel?" he mused. "A thousand times, no!" The vast expected increase in world population and in the number of illiterates worldwide troubled Phil. What was God's answer? Suddenly he knew: *radio*!

In 1960, there were already some twenty-five missionary radio stations, and all were eager for suitable programmes in English and other languages. A well-known authority had recently said: "You folk in WEC are just the people for the Lord to use in this work. Your international links and linguistic abilities in over forty countries fit you for this and the necessary follow-up work."

At the same time came news of the vast increase of the availability of receivers, not only throughout Europe, east and west, but also in Africa where "nationals are reported to be buying radios before shoes!" as well as in Latin America, India and the Far East.

"Neither God nor the radio wave recognises any 'curtain', whether iron, bamboo or of any other material," Phil declared with energy. "Shortly after His resurrection, Jesus often appeared in the midst of His people having passed through walls and doors as if they did not exist. Today God has given the Church the means whereby the news of a Risen Saviour can penetrate the thickest wall or to the remotest village. In one hour, more people can be reached by radio than Paul was able to preach to in a lifetime."

Radio had the great advantage of speaking to people as individuals, not merely as part of the masses. God had commanded His people to reach all *individuals* to the uttermost part of the world with the good news of salvation. If God has commanded something, He must have provided the means by which it could be done. "Paul used ink, parchment, ships, runners, horses and a basket," Phil summarised, "by all means and with all means. Then God gave printing. And now He has given the slim fingers of *radio* and television – and we mustn't let the enemy be quicker off the mark than the Christians!"

In May 1961, Phil's dynamic presentation of his vision for creating "Radio Worldwide" as a new branch of WEC convinced the WEC International Leadership Conference; and he and his wife Mim were commissioned to this new ministry.

The birth of the new baby found the Booths with a desk, a typewriter, a few stamps, a vision . . . and not a clue as to how to proceed, nor where! There followed a year of seeking advice, listening to others, probing means and methods, learning what radio was all about . . . and waiting on the Lord. Other couples were meanwhile being called to join the team.

Suddenly things took off. From a house in SE London, they commuted several times a week to a studio that had become available for recording. Ideas burgeoned; a fine Tamil-speaking Indian Christian joined them, and two major series of programmes were put on the air.

An Indian listener wrote: "Yesterday, I was a Hindu. I listened to your first broadcast, and today I am a Christian and know it!"

The first cry of the new-born baby, "Radio Worldwide", had been heard.

1962 – Pressing full steam ahead

During the WEC Leadership Conference in 1961, there had been a unanimous realisation of the mission's need for its own printing press. The cults and the communists were flooding the newly literate world with their give-away literature, and the Christian Church was lagging far behind.

Though no one present knew anything much about printing, all knew that their ignorance did not greatly worry their all-knowing God! All He needed was their willingness to co-operate.

Neil Rowe, who had been doing four-colour work in Glasgow, had just taken a short course of instruction in printing. He and his wife were duly released from their commitments to the Bible College in Glasgow in order to concentrate on building up this new department. Some money became available to acquire a second-hand lithographic machine. Four students at the College had a burden for such a ministry. Suddenly the whole idea snowballed!

Along with the Glasgow staff, the growing team sought the Lord on such matters as efficient equipment, committed personnel, adequate accommodation and, by no means least, the necessary skill and wisdom to take the first nervous steps in this new field of service. Three thousand and five hundred pounds was received, earmarked for "a WEC printing work, to be based in the Glasgow area". Kilcreggan Convention Centre opened its doors so that the "press" could move in with them.

"We felt so helpless and hopeless," wrote Neil, "but we knew that it was impossible for God to fail."

With a group of volunteer students from the Bible College, they converted the Kilcreggan Estate Lodge into a compact working unit, and moved in "lock, stock and barrel", in January 1963. The four would-be printers had gone to the mission headquarters to be trained and accepted into the ranks as full-time missionaries.

The team was ready to launch out in faith, to discover their way forward by trial and error. They were only too well aware that any step forward would not be achieved by their own ingenuity, but only by the power of the Holy Spirit. Having started with offset printing, they had to make a huge jump into a big production programme, for within two months *Soon*, *Young Warrior* and *Bientôt* (to be followed very quickly by *Cedo* and other language editions of the Gospel Worldwide broadsheets) were due to roll off the presses.

The team worked for over four years in that initial location, developing in skill and ability, producing field and survey material, pamphlets and brochures.

When the British headquarters of WEC moved from Highland Road in Upper Norwood, South London, to Bulstrode at Gerrards Cross, in Buckinghamshire, they asked Neil and Mary Rowe, who were the leaders of the WEC press, to accept the responsibility for administration and development of the new property. As they stepped out of the press team, God had prepared David and Nettie Matthews to step into their place.

The printing press, having outgrown its Kilcreggan premises, was then invited to move south into available space at the new headquarters. New equipment was constantly being added, and the newest techniques learned and practised. Millions of gospel broadsheets in various languages for distribution all over the world, as well as magazines, booklets, leaflets in English and in many other languages, were being printed to help in spreading the gospel wherever WEC missionaries were at work. Posters, charts, Sunday School aids, primers for reading classes – anything that could be used by the Lord to further the spread of the gospel – were printed at basic cost to help forward the aim of the mission, "To reach the remaining unreached people in the shortest possible time."

After the press moved to its spacious new premises at

Bulstrode, things began to move forward at an ever accelerating pace. One thousand hymn books had been printed in Kilcreggan for the Hrey people in Vietnam: a request for a 10,000 edition of a hymn book for Indonesia now followed on its heels! At the same time came exceptional reports from Hong Kong of the use of and need for *Soon*. From Portuguese Guinea came marvellous reports of the ministry of *Cedo*. From Fred Chapman in Worthing came a demand for 174,000 copies of *Bientôt*.

"Why does WEC need its own press?" David was asked. "One reason is that our missionaries find it impossible to get their printing done elsewhere, such as these hymn books for revival-blessed Indonesia," he replied. "Crusaders in Chad, Ghana, France and Ivory Coast have all asked us to help them, as there are few people willing to typeset a foreign language, let alone hymns and their tunes!

"Secondly," he continued, "it is generally cheaper to print for ourselves. A firm quoted one WEC department £110 for a brochure. By using our oldest semi-retired machine and working a little overtime, we managed to do it, despite a very full programme, for seventeen pounds!"

From then on, it truly was a case of *pressing* full steam ahead!

1963 – Can we match their sacrifice?

"On the night of July 3rd, 1963, a band of communist soldiers raided a mountain village of Bru tribesmen just three miles from us," wrote Roy Spraggett. "Their mission was to abduct Tanong, a twenty-five-year-old Christian tribesman." The motive was clearly to terrorise those who believed the gospel and who were associated with the missionaries.

"Two men stole into Tanong's house", Roy went on, "and bound him before he had time to awake. As they led him away into the dark, the leader explained to the terrified tribesmen that Tanong was 'not a good influence'."

As Tanong disappeared into the night, his young wife ran sobbing after him. Angrily, one of the communists turned on her, threatening to shoot her if she did not return home. Would Tanong ever return to her and their baby son? Would he be sent to one of North Vietnam's cruel prisons to be tortured and brain-washed?

Tanong was not the first to be abducted. Dependable, faithful, hard working Yong had been whisked away. Then Oi, the Spraggetts' valuable language teacher, was kidnapped while out fishing.

The Spraggetts visited Tanong's family the moment they received the news of his kidnapping. As they climbed up into his small match-box-like house, Tanong's old mother tried to greet them with a smile but broke down into a terrible sob. His wife sat staring out across the jungle-covered hills, nursing her eighteen-month-old son. The Spraggetts presented the customary gifts for such a sad occasion, and sat down to hear the whole story from Tanong's brother.

As he finished, the young wife turned to them, her face marred by prolonged weeping. They wanted to comfort her but at first no words could pass the lump in their throats. They sought to pray with them for Tanong and Yong and Oi, asking God to sustain them through every trial and cause them to triumph.

"These three precious seeds have fallen into the ground, and they will, they must, bring forth a harvest. They are not lost to themselves, their families or the work," Roy wrote, "but rather they will be the means of gain. They have been counted worthy to suffer for Christ and shall enjoy His reward." Then he added: "This challenge comes to us: *can we match their sacrifice?*"

Just six months later, at 5.30 a.m. on January 7th, 1964, at Cam Phu, while Roy, Daphne and two-year-old Jennifer

Spraggett were still asleep, a terrific explosion shattered their little home. The communists had sought to blow them out of existence because of their support for the Vietnamese and tribespeople of the area.

Neighbours rushed to drag the missionaries from the blazing ruins, finding them severely burned and wounded. It was a miracle that the whole family had not been killed outright. Because of the cold, the baby had not been in her cot that night, but had crept into bed between her parents. Otherwise she would surely have died.

Everything they possessed in this world had gone. Passports and papers were burned to a cinder. Practically nothing could be salvaged from the burnt-out shell of what had once been their home.

More help arrived two hours later, and the Spraggetts were moved to the provincial capital, where American army surgeons gave all possible first aid treatment. Then they were flown to the US Army Field Hospital at Nha Trang. It was some time before they were fit enough to be transferred to a hospital in Saigon, and longer still before they were able to fly to England.

Was the day of missionary work over for Vietnam? Emphatically no! Just a couple of months later, Dr Stuart Harveson wrote of the baptism of seventy-seven believers, including "converted sorcerers, drug smokers and drunkards". Gordon Smith told of the arrival of another twelve orphans. "Where is my mother?" whimpered a little Katu tribes-child, whose parents had been killed in the warfare. The twelve children had been picked up among the dead and wounded, and the American soldiers brought them to the one remaining place where they would be loved and cared for.

So the missionary work continued, despite the raging war. The missionaries knew they still were needed; the God who had taken them out there had not yet told them to return home.

1964 – The "Simba" uprising

Little news filtered through from the war-torn Congo after the guerilla forces, loyal to the murdered Patrice Lumumba, rose up in August 1964 to fight against the national army, loyal to President Kasavubu. The world at large heard of the "Simba" uprising, and all presumed that the foreigners, including thirty WEC missionaries, still in the north-eastern province of the Congo were being held as hostages. No letters came out. Silence reigned.

During November, after three months of captivity, first Jim and Ida Grainger, then group after group of others made their escape by one means or another. Each had differing tales of brutality, and yet also wonderful stories of God's intervention.

Mary Harrison, with broken bones and shattered body, and Joy Taylor with her four wounded children, were rescued in December and they brought news of the martyrdom of Joy's husband, Cyril, and of Miss Muriel Harman.

On the last day of the year came the rescue of all but one of the remaining white WEC "hostages", and with them, news of the martyrdom of Bill McChesney and Jim Rodger. Of Winnie Davies there was still no word.

Cyril and Joy Taylor, with their four children, and Muriel Harman and Mary Harrison were all at Lowa, in that fateful October of 1964. Arrested, Cyril and fourteen-year-old Murray, their wrists brutally tied behind their backs, were thrown on an active ant-hill; they underwent hours of agony at the mercy of the termites. Muriel Harman suffered a great deal of "Simba punishment", which had to be endured to be understood. Hustled aboard a motor launch, the whole party were taken down river to Ponthierville, where they were stripped almost naked, beaten and brutalised, by the local garrison of guerilla soldiers.

On to Stanleyville and imprisonment, along with nuns

and priests, in an underground dungeon on the left bank of the great Zaïre river. Mary fell three feet down a manhole on to a cement floor, breaking her thigh. The rebels then kicked her in the face and chest, breaking her jaw and ribs.

During the deliverance of the city by Belgian para-troopers on November 24th, 1964, a mortar shell whined overhead and landed outside their dungeon-prison, killing ten rebels instantly. In blind anger, a guard rushed into the court-yard, slashing open the heads of Joy's two little girls and her own arms and legs, as they walked in the fresh air.

Hearing their screams, their father rushed up to them, and dragged them back downstairs, where nuns tore up their clothes to stem the terrible bleeding. Desperate for reprisals, other rebels swarmed in and ordered everyone upstairs, leaving Mary and Joy with the two little girls, apparently bleeding to death, down in the darkness. Lined up against the walls, all the prisoners were mown down with machine-gun fire. Joy's two young sons, Murray and Barry, feigned death with the rest. Eventually they crept out from under the dead body of their own father, and back down to their mother, to tell her that "Daddy has gone to be with Jesus!"

Young Murray then prayed with great earnestness that God would send them water and someone to heal and care for his mother and two young sisters. He ended his prayer: "Lord, please forgive the men that shot my Daddy: they didn't know what they were doing!" Two days later, they were found and rescued and flown out to safety and recovery.

American Bill McChesney had been out in the Congo only four years, when the savage "Simba" regime took over. From the outset, the missionaries were left in no doubt that the bitterest hatred of the rebels was reserved for Americans and Belgians.

Marched off from Ibambi, Bill was taken to Wamba, where he was imprisoned with quiet forty-five-year-old Jim

Rodger, a Scot. Bill, cruelly beaten, became a very sick man. When the news came through that Stanleyville had been recaptured, and nearly 2,000 white prisoners rescued, the rebels' anger erupted. Bill and Jim were lined up with the priests and planters of the area for interrogation. Belgians were to be shot, clubbed to death, or their hands tied and hurled alive into the river. For American Bill, they reserved the full fury of their pent-up hatred: but Bill's spirit was already with his Saviour, and nothing but his mortal remains suffered the final degrading savagery.

Schoolmaster Jim, gold medallist and honours-degree holder from Edinburgh University, loved Bill, and nursed him with a mother's gentleness during the last two weeks of his life. He was standing, supporting Bill in his arms, when the last commands were given for Belgians and Americans to remain on the right, and all others to move to the left. Jim stood still. Asked his nationality, Jim said nothing, letting it be assumed that he was an American. A Belgian Roman Catholic priest, about to die, shouted out that Jim was British, but the forgiving minute had passed.

"There is a Friend that sticketh closer than a brother;" but there are brothers who bear something of His likeness. Such were Jim and Bill. They were lovely and pleasant in their lives, and in death they were not divided. Side by side with the New Year's Honours List, the world read the short account of Jim's last words: "I must stick with Bill!"

1965 – The challenge of a National

In 1959, Heini Germann-Edey saw in a vision, young Indonesian people being trained in evangelism, and through their witness the orthodox but dead churches of Indonesia becoming alive and revived. As a direct result of this vision, the Batu Bible College came into being, Pak Octavianus being one of the very first students.

Born in a humble home on the island of Roti, left fatherless when three months old, Octavianus had to work hard from an early age. He came to the Lord as a young lad, and early learned to love the Bible. A missionary, seeing the potential in him, enabled him to go to school, to college and later to the Batu Bible College.

Some years after completing his training, Pak Octavianus became the first Indonesian Principal of this Bible College, where he helped to bring together a dedicated staff of Indonesians, Chinese and Westerners. A five year theological and missionary training course was developed, with practical work playing a major role. Students go to all parts of the archipelago in evangelistic and pastoral teams as a part of their training. Dead churches throughout Indonesia were revived through the ministry of these teams; unreached areas were evangelised, and new churches were established.

One of the results of all this was the Bandung Crusade.

A Bible College team visited this university city for a campaign, at the invitation of fifty-two churches. The Lord so blessed this effort that the local churches were encouraged to make a greater effort later in the year to reach thousands more. They again invited the Batu Bible College students, under the leadership of their Principal, Pak Octavianus.

Tremendous preparation was put in, bombarding the whole city, area by area, with gospel meetings and literature. The churches became united and their members trained in counselling. Special student meetings were arranged in this city where 40 per cent of the population were under twenty years of age. In the last few weeks, a prayer conference was convened, to undergird the whole Crusade with a massive infrastructure of believing prayer.

Led by school bands, the Crusade opened with a Testimony for Christ Parade, with 2,500 children marching through the city streets, carrying Scripture texts. Thirty-five thousand people streamed into the stadium the first night. A government representative declared: "We are in favour of this gospel movement. It is just what we need. In physics there is a rule that nothing can remain empty. This movement must fill the empty spaces in Indonesia with the good news which would otherwise be filled by the bad spirits of Satan."

Despite early restlessness, 500 responded to the appeal the first evening, among them the nephew of the Sultan of Makasser: and he had come only to oppose the preaching! That was the start of a remarkable Crusade. Before its conclusion, approximately three thousand people came forward, under the influence of powerful Holy Spirit preaching, to confess their sins and receive forgiveness from God.

One night, four "crossboys" in leather jackets waited for Pak Octavianus as he left the platform, to say: "Sir, we want to accept the Lord Jesus!" A sixty-five-year-old man had been bedridden for five years, crippled and dumb. He came for healing, but was challenged that first he must receive the Lord Jesus Christ as his Saviour, by repentance and confession of sin. As soon as he had done this, he was wonderfully healed!

Another man, who had found Christ in the preliminary campaign, brought one of his best friends. This man sat with his hands tightly clenched throughout the meeting, mumbling to himself, "I can't go!" He had promised his mother on her death bed that he would never become a Christian, and that he would faithfully continue family devotions in their home around his thirty idols. "No, I can't, I can't!" he cried. "No, you can't," his friend agreed, "but the Lord Jesus can, and He will set you free!" He went forward and found peace at the Cross.

In a great crescendo of praise, the last great day of the Crusade came. School bands again led the amazing march of witness, as 50,000 people gathered in the stadium, all singing "Onward, Christian Soldiers", wet-through but gloriously happy. Tears of joy from thousands of thankful hearts mingled with the raindrops as, sitting on the sodden grass, they watched the masses of schoolchildren doing intricate figure marching.

Through seemingly endless preliminaries, the patient

crowd sat on, until the last message blazed forth. Before the altar call could be properly given, nearly one thousand people streamed to the front, kneeling on the wet grass to surrender to Christ.

In an after-meeting for all who had taken any part in the Crusade, Pak Octavianus challenged them with a strong call to commitment to *mission* – the evangelisation of all Indonesia (their Judaea), all Asia (their Samaria), all Africa (their uttermost parts of all the earth). "Yes; the evangelisation of the *whole world* is *your* task and *mine*," he cried in ringing tones. "We are the largest Church in the Orient, and therefore have the greatest responsibility to other countries." They listened round-eyed, as, for the first time, they saw their responsibility for world evangelisation. And over three hundred responded to the appeal, surrendering their lives to be used in the spread of the gospel.

1966 – "They went over, the trumpets sounding!"

Ron Davies had heard Jock Purves and Rex Bavington speak of the spiritual need of the people of Central Asia, and knew that was where God wanted him. He sailed for India, and spent many years journeying in Baltistan and on the Afghan frontier, living closely with the people. From them, he picked up the language, inflections and manner-isms in a remarkable way. Called up during the war to serve in the Indian army, many commented on his Christian character and the loveliness of his life.

Back again in Northern Kashmir, the part of the world he loved the best, Ron was staying with the three lady workers and they were planning the future development of their work, when rumours of another war reached them. Pathans had entered the land to take revenge on Sikhs who had committed outrages further south. Lorries in great num-bers and at great speed began pouring through the village of

Buniyar, piled high with Sikh families fleeing from the atrocities of the Pathans. Ron managed to hire a pony trap at great cost, and, reassuring the ladies, he bundled them up into the trap with warm clothes and blankets, promising to follow later on foot. Off they went, and Ron in all his simple greatness stood smiling, waving them goodbye.

Wanton butchery was handed out by the conquering Pathans to whoever they met who would not repeat the Qualima, stating that, "There is no God but Allah and Muhammed is his prophet." And later that same day, Ron was thus challenged. Quietly but staunchly refusing their request, he went to be with his Saviour, rather than deny the Lord who had died to save him.

John Haywood left the Mission village of Da Nang at six on Saturday morning, January 8th, 1966, to drive along the main coastal highway to Hue, where he hoped to collect some livestock for the leprosarium farm.

Crossing over the pass, John was following some military vehicles loaded with rice. They had just begun the descent when they were ambushed. John was caught in the middle of the skirmish. Hiding in a metal culvert under the road, he was gunned by a Viet Cong guerrilla, who was hidden in the grass at the other end of the culvert.

When the news reached back to Da Nang, his wife, Simone, responded very quietly: "We committed the trip to the Lord this morning before John left." Later she declared: "John's death does not alter God's call."

On January 13th, Jacqueline Edith was born to Simone, and together, mother and daughter continued in the task to which God had called John and Simone some years before, first in Vietnam, and later in Switzerland.

"Clutching her Bible, she staggered at the head of the rebel column." So the Reverend Father Alphonse Strijbosch, a Dutch Roman-Catholic missionary, described the last hour for Winnie Davies. It was during a vain attempt by the Simba guerrillas to escape the Congolese troops. After the skirmish, Winnie was beyond the reach of further suffering. General Ngalo had killed her and fled. It was May 27th, 1967.

She had sailed for the Congo in 1946, where she worked for some years at Nebobongo, before being invited to go south to begin medical work at Opienge. After the evacuation at the time of Independence, she returned to Opienge, the church there promising to protect her and care for her, whatever dangers lay ahead.

In August 1964, the Simba rebels took her into captivity, and she spent thirty-four long months in their hands. Throughout her captivity, Winnie continued to serve all who needed her skill as nurse or as midwife, irrespective of their creed or politics. General Ngalo gave her his patrimony and a certain amount of protection from the usual crudity of the soldiery, but her health deteriorated, and she found it more and more difficult to keep up with the guerrillas on the long forced marches.

"We marched for three days without food," Father Strijbosch reported of the last few days, "save for a little elephant meat at the end of the march. At dawn of the fourth day, a fresh start was made by the column with Miss Davies at its head. I was at the end as I could not keep up any longer. I had crossed two rivers and was lost in a maze of buffalo and elephant tracks. Suddenly I saw Miss Davies. At first I thought she was resting, being exhausted by the long marches through the jungle. Then I saw . . ." and with a sob, he described what he saw, and how he realised that she was dead. "It must have been fifteen minutes since she had been killed."

Winnie's last message at WEC Headquarters in London, just before returning to the Congo in 1961, had been based on Philippians 1:20, "It is my eager expectation and hope that I shall not be at all ashamed, but with full courage, now as always, Christ will be honoured in my body, whether by life or by death."

1967 – Genesis: Exodus: *Promised Land*

The "Genesis" of WEC took place at No. 17, Highland Road in Upper Norwood, London. Just before he sailed for Africa with Alfred Buxton, C. T. Studd, with considerable foresight, bought this desirable fourteen-roomed house as a home for his wife and daughters. It was here that the mission was born and that the first four staff members set up its home-end headquarters. Canadian, American and Australian headquarters were subsequently opened, helping to house WEC's growing childhood. Nos. 33 and 34 in Highland Road were added to No. 17 in the United Kingdom, and then by the heroic teamwork of candidates, under the guidance of "Uncle Hoppie", No. 19 came into being to cope with the needs of the mission's adolescence. New Zealand, Germany and Switzerland all opened headquarters, but, nevertheless, the adult mission was becoming so prolific that further enlargement was urgently required.

When the British WEC was served with a Compulsory Purchase Order by the Lambeth Borough Council in 1963, the leadership were compelled to make the difficult decision to move headquarters. Lionel Hemmings, Norman Singleton and Ken White, three good friends of the mission, began the long search for suitable accommodation, with sufficient space for all the headquarters' personnel and activities. They travelled over one thousand miles around Greater London in the next three years, in an apparently fruitless search.

During these years, the WEC Press outgrew its accommodation in Kilcreggan. The WEC Youth programme was outgrowing the available space in the Midlands Headquarters. The International Office, with all its personnel, needed proper quarters; and unknown to the mission at the time, God was looking ahead to the needs of the Missionary Orientation Centre. WEC worldwide were believing for an increase in candidates, an ever larger number of whom were married with children. As the mission continued to grow, there would obviously be more and more missionaries on furlough, needing at least temporary homes.

Suddenly, "Bulstrode" was put on the market. The vast, grandiose-looking mansion in its acres of grounds was considered to be of equal value to the properties being vacated, with allowance being given for essential repairs and renovations, reinstatement compensation and legal costs. However, its *real* value to the mission, housing *all* the headquarters staff and their families under one roof, with grounds for camps and halls for weekend conferences, quietness and beauty for refreshment for missionaries on furlough, in close proximity to Heathrow airport as well as to Central London, was inestimable.

The choice that was forced on the staff, realising the fantastic amount of work that would be involved in such a move, yet recognising the tremendous asset that such a property would bestow on the mission, demanded much prayer as they sought God's mind. But eventually, God gave them full peace that this was His choice for them, and so an agreement was reached to buy the property and to move the headquarters.

The planned "Exodus" looked utterly daunting. Months of hard labour were needed, to prepare Bulstrode to receive the invasion. The place was filthy in the extreme; the kitchens needed completely modernising; a central heating system had to be installed; 114 rooms needed decorating and furnishing; eight departments had to be given office space; a nursery needed to be equipped for the many children; garages needed reconstructing. There was seemingly no end to the jobs that would have to be done, while keeping all the normal activities of a busy head-quarters running smoothly. Finally, to move the whole organisation within a week from the south-east to the west of the great metropolis demanded a fantastic dovetailing of hundreds of individual efforts.

"The gigantic move to the Promised Land is completed," was the caption to a brief article in the December 1967 magazine, continuing with the somewhat amusing comment: "All departments are disrupted, so please be prayerfully patient if you are awaiting attention in any matter." Seeing the "before and after" photographs one could hardly be surprised if some letters went astray!

1968 – Tomorrow's Leadership

Christian Student Societies have always been used by God for the extension of the gospel. The English Reformation began when students met in secret at Cambridge to study the banned Greek New Testament. The Methodist revival had its beginnings in the "Holy Club" at Oxford, where the young Wesleys and Whitefield used to meet. The birth of foreign missions in North America can be traced to the Haystack Prayer Meeting at Williams College, where in 1806 Samuel Mills formed a band of students for prayer, whose object it was to "effect in the person of its members a mission to the heathen". And so one could go on.

"The students of today are the national and spiritual leaders of tomorrow," someone has rightly said. They must be won for Christ. Eric Fife declared that students either run a country or ruin it.

In *Japan*, by 1968, there were almost one thousand universities and colleges with one and a half million students. Most of the outstanding leaders of the land in business and politics were graduates of the top universities. Ken and Betty Roundhill were convinced of the essential value of missionary work among these young people. They joined the full-time staff of the Japanese branch of the International Fellowship of Evangelical Students (IFES). Through English Bible Classes, preparation of study material, helping at a weekly meeting for the student Christian leadership, they sought every means to stretch out a hand of friendship. In some colleges, where it was not permitted to hold meetings on the campus, the Roundhills opened their home to the students.

In *India*, it was an apparently casual remark in 1962 that set off a significant chain reaction. A friend remarked to

Ken and Racile Getty that he had rented a bungalow in the hills for a month. "We shall only need it for ten days," he added, "for our student camp. Why don't you have a similar camp there?"

Nestled among pine and deodar trees in the Himalayan foothills, Ranikhet was an ideal situation for a summer students' camp. Despite fears that the students might not be willing to go so far or to pay their own way or to accept the spiritual emphasis of the camps, they came, and have continued to come year after year. Many found the Saviour there, some from Muslim backgrounds, some Hindu, some atheistic. Young believers were established in their faith, and returned to their colleges to witness fearlessly for the Lord Jesus Christ.

"The word 'student' has become a synonym for violence," wrote Alastair and Helen Kennedy, WEC Crusaders also working with the IFES among French-speaking students in *West Africa*. It was 1968. From Tokyo, Surabaja, Rome, Paris, Berkeley and Dakar, there were reports of unrest, rioting, sit-ins and other forms of student protest. In Dakar, the student strike had been timed to start on the first day of the University exams, and led to military intervention with tear-gas, rifle butts and clubs. Some students were killed, many injured, and extensive damage was done to fine buildings.

"It was heartbreaking," wrote Alastair, "to see the damage done, and the campus being taken over by the troops. The twenty members of the little Christian Union, who, just a few hours before the start of the strike, had been having their weekly Bible Study, are now scattered far and wide, and most will probably never return to Dakar.

"In the vital sphere of Christian service in Africa," Alastair continued, "there are peculiar problems to be faced. The enormous distances make it very costly to hold student conferences. Political uncertainty as in places like Brazzaville, Lagos or Cotonou, which can upset travel plans and make the obtaining of visas very difficult is another hazard. Student strikes led by a handful of militants, as witnessed in Dakar, can throw all well-laid plans into confusion.

"However, the challenge and opportunities of this work greatly outnumber the problems" Alastair concluded. "We have seen clearly the tremendous power and influence that can be wielded in a university by a small group of dedicated, well-organised and fearless students: the unrest and violence was forced on the unwilling majority by a militant minority. If troublemakers can do this, cannot we believe that a relatively small group of Christian students with the same fearless dedication to their message could influence as many for Christ?"

Part Four

FELLOWSHIP

1969–1987

It has been a conviction with us for thirty years that the healthiest and most scriptural form of leadership in a work of God should be a spontaneous product from within rather than something imposed from without or above.

Our somewhat autocratic leadership of the first twenty years was God's necessary pattern for firmly fixing the mission in its first three supporting principles of sacrifice, faith and holiness.

Now there has to be the incorporating of the principle of FELLOWSHIP, right into the warp and woof of leadership as well as all other levels of mission activities. The mind of Christ is expressed through the workers themselves; the commissioned are the ones best fitted to interpret as well as carry out the commission. This method of fellowship leadership is only possible to us because the entire WEC staff, at home as well as overseas, consists of full-time workers, whether office, domestic, or itinerant, husbands and wives alike, all tested and welcomed into the Crusade in the same way.

So wrote Norman Grubb, the International Secretary of WEC, in the fifties. Now at the close of the sixties, yet another aspect of fellowship was to be realised in the mission – that of international oneness, as much as interdenominational oneness – as South American, African, Indian, Indonesian, Malaysian, Japanese, Korean and Chinese Christians became fellow-workers and took their rightful place in the ranks of serving missionaries worldwide: the *whole* Church to the *whole* world.

"In Christ there is no east or west"

In Christ there is no east or west,
    In him no south or north,
But one great fellowship of love
    Throughout the whole wide earth.

In him shall true hearts everywhere
    Their high communion find,
His service is the golden cord
    Close-binding all mankind.

Join hands, then, brothers of the faith,
    Whate'er your race may be;
Who serves my Father as a son
    Is surely kin to me.

In Christ now meet both east and west,
    In him meet south and north,
All Christlike souls are one in him,
    Throughout the whole wide earth.

John Oxenham (1852–1941)
Reproduced by permission of
Desmond Dunkerley

1969 – "New wine needs new wineskins"

"From May 25th, until June 21st, WEC leaders from home bases and fields will be meeting in conference at Bulstrode," read the brief announcement.

This was to be a historic gathering of the Leaders' Council, the highest court of appeal in the mission and the guardian of its principles and policies. According to the constitution, this Council meets only in times of grave crisis. In the fifty-six years of WEC's history, it had never yet met in an official corporate way.

What emergency triggered this assembling in 1969? There was none! But the combined weight of a number of very important and relevant matters made it imperative. The strong winds of change blowing through the national and international affairs of the world had not left the churches untouched. Every aspect of witness, worship and growth had been subject to detailed scrutiny in the context of the new day. Missionary societies could not expect to be exempt from these winds of change.

"We thank God that we are not meeting", wrote Norman Grubb, then WEC's International Secretary Emeritus, "because there is some crisis of dissension or faintest breath of desire to change our foundation principles. However, new wine needs new wineskins. Abraham's son was a product of Abraham's faith; but fourteen years later, he was told to sacrifice Isaac, and he obeyed. In faith, he had to believe that God would work a miracle of resurrection into his only son, the son of the promise. In such manner, we in WEC want to be ready to catch the vision. Maybe WEC will be called to 'die' to some of its old forms (as a Western missionary society) and to be resurrected in a new form, seeing our national brethren of many lands becoming the world's missionaries of the future."

Thirty-eight countries and eight hundred missionaries were represented by seventy-six delegates. From start to finish, there was a wonderful spirit of unity. During the month-long conference, the wording of the "Principles and Practice" of the mission was chiselled into present-day sharpness; whole new concepts were added to convey adequately the missionary task of the seventies. There were certain delicate matters (aptly referred to by one delegate as "potatoes of uncertain temperature") that had to be handled with much care and thoughtfulness. This called for unhurried discussion, thorough searching of the Scriptures and time to seek the Lord's mind in prayer, until there was a united sense of knowing the mind of the Lord.

The paramount factor with regard to the future development of the work was the recognition of national Christian leaders as co-partners with the expatriate missionaries. Together, in this century, they must seek to proclaim the gospel to all the remaining unreached peoples.

Pak Octavianus, Principal of the Batu Bible College, and Pastor Idoti Matthias of the Church in Zaïre (formerly the Congo), two "sons of WEC", took their full part in all the discussions, deliberations and decision-making of the conference. This was the first time that national brethren had been so invited into full partnership with the Western missionaries.

The total integration of national and foreign workers in the Batu Bible College in Java, Indonesia, was a tremendous challenge to all other fields. It was realised that identical methods could not always be used in other places, but the spirit of transparent oneness and mutual sharing among Indonesian, Japanese, German and British staff spoke volumes to all the conference delegates.

"While all too conscious of the gaps in our ranks," Ken Roundhill, conference secretary, summed up, "the Holy Spirit challenged us not to sacrifice depth for area; not to worry about our special image, nor to aspire to one that pleases all; to call for no loyalty to an organisation other than the team-work that should spring spontaneously from devotion to Christ Himself; to be more concerned about true unity in the Spirit than the mere appearance of harmony; to avoid making fundamental what is essentially incidental; and to encourage such child-like faith in the Lord Jesus Christ, that neither ourselves nor our praying friends will be over-surprised if the Holy Spirit does more and more wonderful things in us, in our circumstances and through the mission as a whole . . .

"We repudiate the 'closed-door complex' in missions. The opportunities to serve abroad today are so vast they tease the imagination! There is an embarrassing amount of room for the traditional missionary approach and pioneer work, but there is also a new dimension of work on the 'frontiers of the Church' as foreigners and nationals enter an integrated ministry. We need to think less about the problems of overly-sensitive nationalism, the diminishing capacity of the traditional sending churches and the brevity of the time left to us – rather, like Joshua of old, we should 'command the sun to stand still', until the spiritual battle is consummated and our God-given commission fulfilled."

1970 – A village visitor

"The baby was born within half an hour of admission," Minnie and Joan wrote from their Middle-eastern maternity centre. "There were no complications. We could not understand why they had come. This was their fifth child, and all the others had been born at home. Furthermore, both the patient and her husband were afraid of us.

"Neither of us expected much reaction as we began to tell them the way of salvation, but the couple listened well, and seemed to drink in the message. The mother repeated over and over the words of a prayer asking for forgiveness and cleansing in the blood of Jesus. When she was discharged, we gave her a 'wordless book' which we had taught her to 'read'.

"Six weeks later, we visited her in her village. 'How

wonderful that you should come to visit us poor bedouin people,' they exclaimed.

"'Do you still have the little book we gave you?' we asked her. 'Yes,' she replied, 'It is here!'

"'Do you remember that we can only pray to God through the Name of Jesus?' Her face was a blank – she had forgotten it all. How can we reach through to them? How will they ever remember, when they only hear once?"

"Everybody in the village was interested," recounted Viggo, a Crusader in Thailand, several thousand miles away from that small maternity work. "A new missionary had arrived at Mr Ban's house. His nearest neighbours were especially interested. They had heard that Mr Ban had become a Christian, but did not fully understand what this meant. So Mr Ban brought his 'CP' missionary into their homes to visit them and tell them a story – something about a New Life. This story was repeated as many times as they wished to hear it. This was good as they could not understand it the first time, and anyway, they forgot so easily. They were so thankful that the 'CP' missionary never got tired of telling the story. Again and again they would sit quietly and listen patiently. For two months this continued. Then Mr Ban's two neighbours accepted Christ as their Saviour."

During this same period, another "CP" missionary was to be found sitting beside Mr Chuay during his working hours, teaching him the Word of God. After work was over, they would together visit the homes of their friends, where they could explain the gospel or teach the Word.

Another of these versatile "CP" missionaries found his way to a group of Thais who had found the Lord and were learning to walk in His ways. They had found the singing difficult, but the "CP" missionary sang beautifully, and was happy to repeat each hymn over and over again, until they were word perfect and reasonably well in tune.

Who were these "CP" missionaries? Who was sending out these effective messengers of the gospel?

In 1968, Viggo Søgaard and Leslie Brierley had experimented with cassette players for the specific ministry of Church building. The multiplication of gifted teachers of the Word by means of electronic machines would help mitigate the great lack of teachers in areas where the spiritual harvest was potentially substantial.

So "Cassette Circles" became a new WEC project in 1970, and the "missionary" a Philips N2200 Cassette Playback machine (known shortly as a "CP"); its only food being torch batteries!

The use of these playback machines began to fill a big gap in the total evangelistic programme of missions and churches. So few new converts were capable of teaching others the basic elements of the Christian faith or of how to become effective witnesses to the Lord Jesus back in their villages. Foreign workers are often responsible for several scattered village churches, and quite unable to spend enough time with any one group to teach them in depth and give them a real grounding in the Word. Then, too, the message needs to be repeated so often before it can be sufficiently understood to change hearts and lives, and there is rarely adequate time for such a ministry.

"I cannot possibly cope with this task," one foreign evangelist wrote. "There are twenty-five groups in my area and no one but myself to teach them."

The revolutionary Cassette Playback was one answer to this need. These "CP" missionaries could witness in the market-place, teach in schools, preach in churches and teach new believers. On one occasion, a couple of these small missionary machines penetrated into the precincts of a Buddhist temple to expound Christian truth!

Within a year, 120 "CP" missionaries were at work in Thailand, and some over the border in Laos. Several new churches had sprung up through their ministry. "Backed up by prayer," wrote one Crusader, "these 'CP' missionaries will be greatly used of the Lord. It is the voice of the Holy Spirit who must speak to the hearts of the people."

Minnie and Joan left a "CP" missionary with that impoverished bedouin couple. They told them again the way of salvation and explained how the cassette would teach them more, and tell them over and over again, as often as they wanted to listen. "We trust and pray that the novelty of being the only ones in the village to have a 'missionary' in their home", the girls wrote, "will cause them to play it often to their neighbours. Only God could have constrained these people to come to us. May He now draw them into a living relationship with Himself."

1971 – The power of the Djoro

"Every seven years there is a ceremony at which all children are initiated into the tribe and dedicated to the worship of Djoro," read a report from Upper Volta in West Africa. "Thus all Lobis are brought under the power of the Djoro. Truly they are a people who sit in darkness."

The Lobi's reputation in West Africa was such that other tribes would not employ them as workmen. "To find work in Ghana we will have to say that we are Dagari and not Lobi," two tribesmen decided together. "If they discover we are Lobi, they will never give us a job!"

They were a proud, independent people, unwilling to submit to authority. Until they had killed someone, they were not considered "he-men". Before the government imposed law and order, it was even considered unsafe for anyone of another tribe to walk through their territory.

One hundred and ninety thousand were scattered throughout Upper Volta (Burkina Faso), sacrificing animals to their mud idols, their lives dominated by the power of Satan. Many were also outwardly bowing to Islam, the religious system which demands much but offers little – no forgiveness for sin, no peace of heart, no assurance for the future. They were a people gripped with an inexplicable resistance to the gospel.

It was in 1934 that Jack Robertson first arrived in the land to bring the gospel to these Lobi tribesmen. He remembers most vividly a wonderful story that still encourages the missionaries in the 1980s to believe that God will break down the fierce opposition in Lobi hearts to the good news of salvation.

In the mid-1940s, a young lad, too small to farm, was sent by his family to watch the cows. With a club over his shoulder and quiver of arrows under his arm, he set off for the grasslands, some way from the village.

A hungry lioness, prowling in the long grass, caught the scent of the cattle and crept up on them unawares. Suddenly, the child tensed as the cows moved uneasily away. Seeing the beast, he sought to defend the herd, throwing first stones and then his club at the crouching lioness. Snarling, the animal sprang – the lad was so small and such easy prey.

Women, hearing the boy's shouts, began to wail: "a lion . . . cows . . . the boy . . ." until the whole village knew. Men ran for their weapons and the hunt was on. Finding her, with the partly eaten body of the boy still in her jaws, they let fly. The maddened beast turned and attacked, mauling four men, before she was killed.

They carried the wounded men to the village of the "white men", to the missionaries who had sought to win their allegiance from idols to the Son of God. With strong iodine and much prayer, they treated the injured men and arranged for them to be transported to the nearest French doctor. Healed and about to return, they were assured by the doctor: "It's not my medicine that saved you. Go and thank your own white men, the missionaries. They saved your lives for you."

Tonhulay Momo, the leper man, was one of those four,

and he became friendly to the missionaries. Had they not saved his life? Out of his poverty, now and again he brought them a gift – and so he began to hear the grandest story that any one man can tell to another, the story of Jesus, who saves men from their sins and from eternal death.

At last the day came when he asked this man Jesus to save his eternal life, as the "Jesus people" had saved his mortal life. One Sunday afternoon, Jack Robertson accompanied him across the marsh to his home, prayed with him for the protection of the powerful Blood of Jesus, and watched him destroy his idols.

There was great consternation in the village. His wife, mother and neighbours ran and hid themselves. Surely the Djoro would strike him dead? However God's hand was on Tonhulay, and he began to grow stronger and more prosperous. With Jack, he built the first church ever founded among the Lobi people, at Bouroum-bouroum.

For more than twenty years he served the Lord gladly and faithfully. Then, in 1971, he was taken ill, and despite emergency surgery, he passed away, singing "There is power in the blood"!

1972 – "Whatever you can do, we can do better!"

"Japan is celebrating the centenary of its first Christian Church," wrote Chandu Ray, in June 1972. Emphasis during the celebrations was to be on the preaching of the gospel to all the people of Japan, and to this end, a congress on evangelism was planned.

"As I heard the talk of Japanese leaders of their role in creating and maintaining freedom and independence of Asian countries, and of sending them on economic missions," Chandu Ray said, "we felt that God was calling the Japanese Christians to lead in the co-ordination of Asians who wish to go out from their own lands as missionaries."

Japan was indeed a highly developed country. Economically, the attitude of the Japanese people of 1972 could be summed up in the slogan: "Whatever you can do, we can do better!" Educationally, Japan had over one million students in her numerous universities and colleges: yet religiously, Chandu Ray knew that only a very few knew the Lord Jesus Christ as their personal Saviour.

Since 1950, Japan had seen the emergence of many new religions of the syncretic type (combining what was considered to be the best of Buddhism, Shintoism, Confucianism and Christianity) as well as the resurgence of several dormant religions and sects, each seeking to fill the spiritual vacuum in the life of the people. The "Soka Gakkai", a politico-religious organisation, was making dramatic gains, trying to satisfy man's desire for quick profit, health and happiness.

But there was another anniversary also being celebrated in 1972. The previous year, WEC, as a missionary agency in Japan, had ceased to exist. The missionaries became fully integrated with the Japanese Church, in what became known as the "Sekai Fukuin Dendo Dan" (SFDD). And 1972 was their first united birthday!

"Reflection on this year", wrote Ken Roundhill, after twenty years of service in the country, "makes us pensive, joyful, sad and encouraged all at the same time." Integration had brought unseen problems and new dimensions to the need for cultural adjustment. The "workers' committee", chaired by the Japanese leader, Pastor Nagasawa, had many Japanese-speaking nationals and twenty-six English-speaking missionaries! There were financial hurdles, as well as linguistic ones, to conquer, but the Lord was definitely and clearly overruling differences and underlining oneness.

The newly formed SFDD was deeply aware that the only answer to man's deepest needs is Christ. He alone can deal with the sin problem and thus lead men to true peace and satisfaction. Already witnessing in five cities and three towns, the Sekai Fukuin Dendo Dan were determined to see real growth and expansion of the Christian Church during the anniversary year of 1972. Eighteen of their young people were already in full-time service, and the Church had almost doubled in the past two years, but all were deeply conscious that it was no time for complacency.

Ken and Betty Roundhill, who met and married in Japan, had been the leaders of the WEC team there from 1959 to 1971, when it was their great joy to hand over leadership to Pastor Nagasawa. The Roundhills stayed on in the newly integrated fellowship, continuing their ministry to the student world.

Then as part of the anniversary celebration, they were invited to set up a training course for Japanese missionaries. "By this time", Ken testified, "there were several missions in Japan with missionaries abroad, but still no training facility in the country. Betty and I agreed to the request, on the understanding that we could train Japanese missionaries from any evangelical society, and not just WEC-related churches." This was totally in line with C. T. Studd's original vision that WEC would be a service mission for any seeking to extend the Kingdom of God.

In the next ten years, they had the joy of training thirty-two Japanese Christians in a "Training Centre" in their own home. The Centre's graduates went out to serve God with different agencies working in fifteen different countries. "The Lord didn't give us children of our own," Betty testified, "but we have a very large 'family', not only in Japan, but now in many other countries where our graduates are ministering." The Uzumasa Church in Kyoto had a young pastor who first heard the gospel in their home when he was a student. Missionary Training Centre students have enlarged the vision of their sending churches all over Japan.

Then the leadership of the Training Centre was passed over into capable Japanese hands. So what now for the Roundhills?

They felt their time of service was not yet ended. They were only in their seventies, they wrote to Pastor

Nagasawa, so surely there must be a job they could tackle to help and serve the Japanese Church?

Yes! They returned once more, in 1987, to set up a Bible School for the churches with whom WEC has integrated. "We would have viewed this project," writes Ken, "with more panic than joy, if it were not for indubitable proof that the Lord has called us back to this task. With Wesley, we know that 'what is commanded is compassable', and so we take courage, and trust that the input from our colleagues will result in a wider ministry than ever for our national brethren."

1973 – "Up, for this is the day"

"Diamond Jubilee Year! Three-score years have passed in the history of WEC – sixty years of advance, change and adjustment, sixty years of ever-widening opportunity, challenge and of proving God's faithfulness. He is the same, yesterday, today and for ever. He does not change. He is as relevant to this generation as to the last. We affirm our faith in God our Commander. We reaffirm our adherence to the principles He has given us. We go forward confidently at His command, 'Up, for this is the day'!"

So began the January magazine 1973 – and every magazine through the year carried backward looks of thankfulness, outward looks of expectancy, forward looks of determination, and upward looks of hope. There were wonderful and detailed surveys from every field and department of all that God had already done through the ministry of the mission, as well as carefully worked-out and prayed-over programmes for advance in every direction.

"Communications" had become an in-word. Radio broadcasting, cassettes, magazines, gospel broadsheets and posters all played their part along with the more old-fashioned yet still deeply effective one to one preaching of the Word. Each part of the vast WEC family sought to communicate what they had done and were planning to do to take the gospel in a meaningful way to yet unreached peoples.

"In presenting the work of WEC over the past sixty years", the magazine editor wrote, "there is the danger of exalting man, mission or method. Therefore we underline that God is the Leader and Commander of this mission and it is to Him we give the glory. It was God who brought the mission into being and it is God who sustains and uses it in His worldwide purposes. He has always chosen to use the weak, the foolish, the lowly and despised, that 'no one may boast before Him' (1 Cor. 1:28, 29).

"We dare not boast", she continued, "of great achievement or rest on past victories. Only as we press forward in humble dependence upon God can we be used to bring a life-giving message to the world. If anything has been accomplished it is because man has been weak enough to let God be strong; foolish enough to let God be wise; as nothing that God might be everything. To Him be the glory."

"The first note to be sounded in this our Diamond Jubilee Year", wrote Robert Mackey, the British Home director, "is one of praise, as we reflect on the great things God has done for us, whereof we are glad. We have grown, developed and expanded organisationally and geographically to the point where it is literally true to say that the sun never sets on the mission. We are still a unity despite the fact that we are now interracial, as well as international and interdenominational.

"From the start, our marching orders were to evangelise the remaining unevangelised peoples of the earth in the shortest possible time. God has enabled us to plant our feet in more than forty lands, and to use every available modern means to fulfil our commission. Response has of course varied from place to place, for some soils are kinder to seed than others. Some areas wait to see their first convert: others have thrived and are now joining the ranks of those countries who are sending missionaries out to propagate the gospel beyond their own borders.

"God has kept us flexible enough to be ready to adjust to new ways. There are the new ministries, to meet modern day needs – the Youth Crusade, Gospel Literature Worldwide, Radio Worldwide, Cassette Circles. There is the new way of total integration with national brethren in the country we serve.

"In this our Diamond Jubilee Year, it is timely to be reminded that milestones are to be passed, not sat on. The glimpse backwards to all that God has graciously enabled to be done should fill us with humble thanksgiving, but it must never be allowed to engender complacency or to breed spiritual inertia. No mission can be satisfied to rest on its laurels nor to be content with former glory or present accomplishments.

"The spur is onwards. There are always other worlds to conquer. We must be willing to be challenged and by faith, to obtain the promises. So let us press forward to those things which are before."

1974 – Europe, the forgotten mission field

In the seventies, Europe was one of the most neglected mission fields in the world, with fewer missionaries among its 500 million people than in the one eastern city of Hong Kong! Vast cities existed in Europe with practically no Christian witness. Thousands of immigrants – Pakistanis, Indians, Arabs; Algerians, Moroccans; Turks and Koreans – presented a mission field of exciting dimensions.

"What better missionary could one hope for", Leslie Brierley wrote, "than a born-again immigrant, called by the Lord to return to his own people and to witness to the gospel?"

So-called Christian Europe has in the present century suffered profound political pressures under the hammer blows of two world wars. The Christian Church has been shaken and split by sectarian struggles. Christian believers and leaders have sometimes found themselves on opposite sides of political frontiers.

Amongst young people, fast becoming the majority in some countries, there is an increasing spirit of discontent: and they protest, sit in, take industrial action, seeking by any means to impose minority rule. Taking to drugs or to the occult, others opt out of the present social structure, feeling it is beyond repair.

In such a setting, the Christian Church has to seek to witness to the Truth as it is in Jesus Christ.

WEC, along with other missions, moved into Spain, with its booming growth in materialism and parallel religious indifference; its young people basically interested in pop music, the opposite sex and a good job with a flat or a car. With a freedom to proclaim the gospel such as has rarely been possible in Spanish history, there is a new openness in the hearts of many, when confronted by living testimony to the power of God. Bible study centres and bookshops, house groups and pastoral ministry are all proving possible in the midst of the concrete jungles.

WEC and others moved into France, with its thousands of towns and villages without a gospel witness, forty million people living outside any religious practice. There are ten times as many communist cells as Bible-believing churches. The old often cling desperately to a religion in which they have lost confidence but which they dare not abandon: the young are drawn to the "isms" of sects and the occult.

WEC moved into Italy, first to Naples, famous for its palaces, castles and churches, and for the beauty of its bay, ringed by steep volcanic hills, but with an underlying vast unemployment problem and economic instability. A local Christian fellowship invited the missionaries to assist in evening Bible School teaching, pastoral care and Sunday School work.

WEC moved into Sardinia. They were joined by a young national, converted in Germany and called by God to be a full-time evangelist to his own people. It was not easy for Antonio and his family to bear the antagonism of their own people. "Visiting from house to house", Antonio wrote, "we noticed great indifference to the gospel. The few who are sympathetic to God's Word quickly become discouraged and hide behind religious hypocrisy." For centuries they have followed the same monotonous forms and ceremonies which are without spiritual life or significance: and it was hard for a Sard to change his habits and customs. Any who frequent the evangelical meetings are labelled traitors to the Roman Catholic religion.

WEC moved in among the Koreans and the Turks in Germany. Derek and Hannelore Earl, who had already worked for years in Korea, had the joy of seeing five of a group of nine Koreans brought to the Lord in their first few months in Germany. Bible conferences, mobile book stores, cassette messages and teaching were all means to reach out to these needy people. Likewise, Jurg and Marlis Heusser from Switzerland moved in amongst the Turks.

WEC moved into the British Midlands, to meet the Indians and Pakistanis, Asian and Arab immigrants, Muslims and Hindus. Turbans and brightly coloured saris; the spicy smell of curries; mosques, temples and guadwaras; Punjabi, Hindi and Urdu languages voiced in arguing, explaining, talking, shouting, clamouring – all belonging to the heat and glare of the exotic East – are now to be found in Britain. Each ethnic group is a people proud of their religion and culture. Drawn together in their communities, their stress is on the importance of family life and the preservation of their national identity. Yet their teenagers are caught between the conservatism of their parents and the "freedom" of their British counterparts at school or college. Bookshops and cassettes, broadsheets and friendliness, weekly meetings and radio broadcasting are helping to bridge the gap between the communities and the Christian missionaries, and to present the true claims of Jesus Christ.

1975 – Senegal River Valley

In December 1975, Neil Rowe and Peter Banfield travelled
up the Senegal River Valley, to see first hand the desperate
need of the people and to hear their appeals for medical
assistance for their sick and fresh water wells for their
agriculture.

"Senegal River Valley" may sound exotic, but how
different are the facts from fiction and fantasy! The river
forms the border between the former French territory of
Senegal (still open to missionaries) and the Islamic Republic of Mauritania (now totally closed to messengers of the
gospel). On the edge of the Sahara, there is a short three-
month season of rains, and nine long months of dryness.
Most of the land is arid and agriculture is at subsistence
level, except along the banks of the river, where thousands
of Senegalese Wolofs and Toucouleurs live, as well as the
trading Maures from Mauritania.

In 1933, WEC had first entered southern Senegal. The
work there had been intensely difficult, the setbacks and
disappointments many, but slowly a church was forming. In
1958, a survey had been undertaken of the Senegal River
Valley 300 miles to the north, and this had become a target
area for the missionaries. In 1963 Peter and Thelma
Banfield entered and settled at Podor, two among one
hundred thousand Muslims. For ten years they struggled
on, a few new workers coming and going, but none staying.
It was tough. Then the Banfields were appointed to
leadership in the Casamance, in south Senegal.

From 1967, Bill and Meg Lapworth and their four boys
had lived for seven years in Mauritania, on the northern
side of the Senegal River Valley, where Bill was employed
by the government to teach national high school students.
They were alone among the one million Maures, all bound
to Islam, with no known Christian among them, let alone a
witnessing Church of Maures. However, in 1974, the day
came that their work permits were rescinded, and they had
to leave the country.

Then during the whole of 1975, there were *no* workers available for the River Valley, neither to the north in Mauritania, nor to the south in Senegal.

In 1976, prayer began to be redoubled for this needy area, asking God for sufficient personnel for the Casamance in south Senegal, so that the Banfields could be released to go north again to the River Valley, plus a minimum of four other workers.

In October 1977, the Lapworths sailed for Senegal, to seek to reach Maures in the River Valley. As personnel became available for the Casamance, they were joined by the Banfields in January 1978, and together the two families established encouraging beachheads. "They have a tough assignment," a visitor wrote, "and any joining them need to be certain of a good old-fashioned call!"

"One day you'll be a missionary like your parents," said an elderly lady. "No, I won't," replied an indignant teenager, "that's the last thing I'll be!"

God must have smiled as He heard Barbara Scott's vehement reply. Barbara grew up at Nebobongo (Congo) where her parents, Arthur and Irene, worked for years amongst the leprosy patients and in training national para-medical personnel. She was twelve years old when she gave her heart to the Lord at the WEC Kilcreggan Conference Centre. Three years later, the Lord challenged her through John 20:21, "As the Father has sent me, even so send I you," and she answered, "Here am I, Lord: send me."

Trained as a nurse/midwife, Barbara did her Bible School training, and during this time, a great burden for Muslims settled on her heart, particularly those in the country of Chad. In October 1977, she sailed for Chad to share the love of Jesus with the needy people of that land.

In February 1979, amongst others, Barbara Scott and co-worker Jenny Carpenter (from Australia) were evacuated from Chad due to heavy fighting. In September, to be

better fitted for future service in Chad, they went to Jordan
for further Arabic language study.

Then, in November 1980, "The Senegal River Valley
team is very encouraged at the arrival of two more nurses to
help in reaching the Muslims in this arid northern area,"
the report ran. "Barbara Scott and Jenny Carpenter
(evacuated from Chad and as yet unable to return there)
are spending a wait-and-see term helping Meg Lapworth in
the clinic. They are excited to find that, by slightly adapting
their Chad Arabic, they are able to communicate with the
hundreds of Mauritanians who come across the river to
trade or settle."

By November 1981, Barbara and Jenny, having learned
the local Wolof language, started applying themselves to
learning Hassaniya in order better to reach the Maures.
They moved into Buntobat, a fishing village at the north
end of Lake Guiers, where 250 Maures lived. Many more
were in surrounding villages and nomadic encampments.
The girls planned to reach them through simple medical
care, sharing their faith at the same time. They knew that
God had now called them to reach the Maures and Senegalese of the River Valley, as surely as He had previously
directed them to Chad.

God was indeed graciously answering the concerted
prayers of the past five years to send a missionary team into
the Senegal River Valley.

1976 – Seed sown must bring a harvest

Lapped by the cool waters of the Gambia River estuary and
shaded by tall palms and flowering frangipanis, the burial
ground of Banjul is a quiet spot outside the city. A simple
stone marks the grave of David Barron.

The Republic of the Gambia is situated on the "bulge" of
West Africa, entirely surrounded by Senegal and the

Atlantic Ocean. It is a fifteen-mile-wide finger of land extending eastwards from the ocean for 200 miles along the lower reaches of the River Gambia. The whole country is low-lying, with thick mangrove swamps at the coast and along the river. Sandy hills rise to the north and south, where the Gambians grow their peanut crops, which comprise the main source of exportable wealth.

There are fewer than half a million people, in five main ethnic groupings, and 95 per cent of them are Muslim.

David and Margaret Barron opened up the work in the Gambia in 1958. After only one year, David died and Margaret returned home, to work at Kilcreggan Conference Centre. A new field had been entered and the work had been started, only to be cut off at its very beginnings.

"We are sure this is not the end of the work," someone prophesied; "God's law of the harvest always works – seed sown must bring a harvest."

God had been burdening others with the need of the Gambia. Two German nurses, Hanna Forster and Maria Robbelen, had heard David and Margaret tell of the medical needs of these people. When God had spoken to Hanna of the Gambia, she had been horrified! "But, Lord, I am not made for pioneer work," she protested. "Maybe a little later?"

God took her at her word. The two young women went to work in Liberia, later joined by Ruth Dieterich. "When news reached me of David Barron's death", wrote Hanna, eight years later, "something within me broke." However, at that time, it was impossible for her to go, as single women were not being invited to the Gambia. Then, in 1965, the Gambia received its independence, and at once the three nurses knew that God had spoken. It was His perfect time.

"In a little hotel room in Banjul," Hanna wrote, "we spent hours in prayer. Then we went to the Minister of Health to offer our services in the name of WEC. The official was a Muslim, but surprisingly kind. We told him that we could only come and work if we were given perfect freedom to preach the gospel. He laughed! 'You can preach the gospel as much as you like,' he said, 'but no one will be converted to your religion.'"

So the application to commence medical work in the Gambia was granted, with full liberty to preach the gospel. The Lord provided a marvellous plot of land, and Hanna's father, a retired architect, built them a home. "But we came to build a church, not a home," Hanna reminded the Lord. "All right," God challenged them, "start a service."

Who would come? Even as they discussed it, there was a knock at the door. Two Muslims stood there. "We heard that you can give us the Word of God." The nurses gave them copies of Mark's Gospel in their own language: and then prayed and sang with them in German, as they had not yet learned enough Mandingo to communicate with them!

The following Sunday, the two men returned with eleven friends. Within ten years, there were 120 attending every Sunday, meeting on the women's verandah. A Church had been born in the Gambia.

The team of workers grew steadily, in a most international way. There were German, Australian, New Zealand, Swiss, Canadian, American and British workers in eight different centres. The medical work was greatly appreciated by the government authorities. Training young men as medical orderlies gave a wonderful opportunity for presenting the gospel and several of them were saved and baptised. In the villages, some were turning to the Lord and burning their witchcraft. A demon-possessed youth was delivered, and many saw and marvelled at the power of God.

WEC also contributed to the government agricultural programme. No one can obtain a visa unless involved in either the medical or the agricultural programme. Doctors and agricultural specialists are still urgently needed to fulfil all the potential, with a wide-open door for effective evangelism.

Seventeen years before, David and Margaret Barron had stood on the deck of the ship as it drew into the harbour at the mouth of the Gambia River and looked expectantly toward the country to which God had called them. Zechariah's song welled up in their hearts as the shoreline drew nearer: "And many nations will be drawn to the Lord . . . and you [Gambia] will know that the Lord Almighty has sent me to you" (Zec. 2:11).

God is indeed fulfilling His promise and doing a wonderful thing in this Muslim land. The "seed sown has brought forth a harvest".

1977 – Patterns in the shadow of the Crescent

"The swarthy unshaven Persians sat cross-legged, chipping away with their little hammers at the paper patterns fixed to the glazed, tile squares," Leslie Brierley wrote in the *Look* missionary news. "One was cutting the outline of a flower on a deep blue tile: another the light blue petals: yet another, the yellow centres. The architect had drawn a beautiful geometric design to cover the walls, domes and minarets of a new theological seminary in the holy city of Qom. Each group of tile cutters was responsible for a small section. Designed by the architect and worked out by the men following his pattern, the finished building would be a beautiful sight."

Islam is working to a pattern traced out for them by the prophet Mohammed. More than a million and a half Muslims visit Mecca every year, an outstanding exhibition of piety and devotion to their God. In 1977, *Newsweek* recorded:

The mood of this year's hadj was one that transcended personal piety. The pilgrimage was a challenge to the world's 700 million Muslims to unite, in law and custom as well as in religious belief, behind a resurgent Islamic fundamentalism with a conservative anti-communist thrust. According to the Qur'an a reform arises within the Muslim world once each century to rekindle the torch of Islam.

The pattern of Mohammed's faith was to be focused more sharply.

"The pattern of Islam's opposition to the Christian gospel", wrote Leslie, "is also becoming more sharply focused. Some countries, such as Saudi Arabia, Libya and Afghanistan, remain fast closed to Christian missionaries. In other countries, increasing restrictions are placed on the activities of Christian foreigners and nationals. In some lands it is forbidden to speak of Christ to a Muslim. To reinforce Islam's impact on Africa and the Western world, centres of Islam are being opened in strategic places – London, Rome, Dakar and Monrovia. Wherever Muslims go, each one is a missionary for his faith, be he a humble kola-nut seller in West Africa or an affluent oil salesman in Europe.

"If only Christians would witness with equal fervour to their faith, and return to the teaching of the Christian Scriptures! There is a pattern clearly visible in the way that Christians in the past have sought to evangelise Muslims: yet the Church has only given lip-service rather than a genuine prayer burden to effect this, for only 2 per cent of career missionaries have gone to Muslim lands. Because we have lacked a clear understanding of the Muslim culture, we have often preached the gospel ineffectively. We have scaled down our goals to our potential rather than seeking to reach them through the strategy and power of the Spirit."

The pattern is at last changing. Younger workers, and the somewhat unexpected offensive of the Muslim community, have shaken the Church out of its complacency. In North Africa, there were more conversions in the seventies than in the previous fifty years. In West Africa, the seemingly impregnable Fula tribe yielded its first-fruits. Kano, the ancient Muslim city of Nigeria, now has its cluster of prospering Christian churches. In Egypt, the Spirit of God is laying hold of influential Muslims and bringing them to the feet of Jesus.

Millions of Muslims now live in lands where Christians are free to reach them. In some Islamic lands, there has been a revival among the Christian minority community, as with the seven million Christian Armenians and Copts among the two hundred million Muslims of the Middle East. Then, too, more young Christians are being trained and mobilised to witness for Christ in other cultures.

"So", concluded the *Look* article, "we see patterns – Islamic patterns, Christian patterns, God's pattern. May the Lord enable us to work with skill at the segment of the pattern which He, the Architect and Builder, puts into our hand. Let us cut according to His pattern with knowledge and with grace, as we keep in mind the beauty of His finished work."

1978 – "Strengthen, lengthen and enlarge!"

Saturday June 3rd, 1978 marked the start of "Intercon '78", an International Conference of WEC leadership to be held at Kilcreggan. By evening, almost one hundred members of the WEC family from all over the world were ready to start.

Much intensive preparatory work had been done. All delegates had received lead-in papers on the main topics for discussion, so that the best possible use could be made of each day of the all too short three weeks allocated to cover a formidable agenda. The aim was to look ahead and to seek to discover God's plan for the whole mission for the coming decade.

The motto for the conference stood out in bold letters above the platform in the meeting room: *Strengthen, lengthen and enlarge!* as Isaiah prophesied to the captive children of Israel, not yet released from Babylonian exile.

> Enlarge the place of your tent, and let the curtains
> of your habitations be stretched out; hold not back,
> lengthen your cords and strengthen your stakes (Isa.
> 54:2).

There was to be a strengthening of the basic principles of
the mission and of the fellowship of all workers: a lengthen-
ing of the cords by a multiplying of the means employed for
the presentation of the gospel to as many as yet unreached
peoples in the world as possible: and an enlarging of vision
and heart and comprehension, to bring in and suitably train
more and more workers for the still unfinished task.

It was an amazing group, representing many cultures and
languages, social and educational backgrounds, as well as
opinions! There were missionaries in their eighties and
others in their thirties: there were national Church leaders
from Japan, Indonesia, India, Zaïre, Liberia, Ghana,
Brazil and Venezuela: there were guests from the Evangelical Missionary Alliance, from the Indonesian Missionary
Fellowship and Bible Institute, and from the Lausanne
Committee for World Evangelisation. There were people
of eighteen different languages from over forty different
countries. And the declared aim was for unanimity on
every subject!

Each day started with an unhurried time for united
worship. Then the agenda business was dealt with, sometimes in plenary sessions, sometimes in small groups and
committees. As the days passed, everyone was increasingly
aware of the deep love and fellowship binding all delegates
together. On all issues, discussions were harmonious, each
willing to hear the other, and to be led into the mind of the
Lord. As one delegate commented, "Had the whole conference been open to public scrutiny, there was not one
moment that would have caused me to blush, not one raised
voice or angry protest." Each delegate had the freedom to
speak out and air different points of view, but always with a
humble spirit, willing to learn from one another. "When we
couldn't agree," one leader said, "we broke off for prayer,

and came back to the subject refreshed in the Lord, for further consideration." The final result was that every decision *was* unanimous!

Delegates were blessed in many different ways. "God showed me", Peter Keevil of Venezuela testified, "that we can disagree yet still walk in the light." "It is one thing to read about things in a book," said Mike O'Donnell, a newcomer to large WEC conferences and from a difficult, often lonely, sphere of service; "another to see it worked out! The idea of a huge multi-mixed fellowship reaching decisions in unanimity, without taking votes or sides – I have now seen it in practice. It really works, when God is in it!"

"It was a blessing to me", wrote Martha Hines, wife of the Colombian field leader, "to see the love expressed even in the chairing of meetings and the serving of meals!"

"God spoke to me clearly," testified Pastor Nonziodani of Zaïre, "and I now have one objective: to see the Church in Zaïre training and sending out missionaries to take the gospel to people of other cultures." Pastor Cesar Rodriguez of Venezuela praised God for bringing him to Intercon '78. "As a result," he said, "I now have a new fire in my heart for evangelism." Liberian Church leader, Donald Wuanti, felt that the greatest blessing he had received was through a message about Philip and the Ethiopian eunuch. "I now understand that God can use ordinary men, who are faithful and obedient, to fulfil His purposes. For the first time, I am able to see beyond the boundaries of my own work, and I thank God that Kilcreggan has broadened my horizons."

"I go back with a better knowledge of the world's need," wrote Pastor Jonathan Santoz of Brazil, "and a burden to see my country doing more towards its evangelisation." No one needed to *hear* a testimony from Pastor Ruichi Nakazawa of Japan, "His smile speaks better than words!" Brother Sarvanand Lall of India, who brought a deeply moving challenge to the conference of the desperate need of hundreds of millions of people in his land, who were dying and going out into a Christless eternity, testified with tears to a deeper devotion to Christ than ever before.

So the great conference ended, and the one hundred delegates went back to their many different spheres of service, the same and yet so different. Heads held higher, eyes sparkling brighter, hearts beating faster, there was a united determination to see God work out His purposes for this dying world of lost sinners, in and through the work and workers of WEC, as never before.

1979 – West goes East: East goes West

Alan was a plumber, Jean was a schoolteacher – two Britishers, both successful in their respective careers. They had met and married, and knew what they wanted of life. It wasn't religion! No shackles, no children: they were too expensive and inconvenient. They would be free – for pleasure, with holidays abroad without financial restrictions or the irritating encumbrance of family responsibilities.

They bought their dream home, and furnished it lavishly. Now a few steps ahead of all the "Joneses" in their street, Alan bought a status symbol, a fast car. They had arrived. What next? Boredom.

They would check out of the rat-race, pull up their roots, travel the world and see how the other half lived. Sights and sounds excited them: the freedom was exhilarating. But dissatisfaction dogged them. The "other half" didn't know what life was about, after all.

Moving on East, Alan and Jean Middleton joined others looking for thrills in the drink and drugs scene. Savings evaporated. Kicks were costly and short lived. Their health broke down – and their marriage. They had lost respect for themselves and for each other. Their children (whom they hadn't even wanted) were just a nuisance to them.

In India, in desperation, they started to delve into oriental cults. A meal and a place to sleep were available in

Buddhist temples. Visiting an Indian bazaar, desolate and hopeless, they were arrested by the consistently radiant life of an Indian tailor. Several times they made their way back to him, where he shone with an inner peace and a purpose in life.

Ramesh Timotheus, the tailor, shared with them his Christian faith, introducing them to missionaries who demonstrated Christ-like love, taking them in and caring for them. First Alan, and then Jean, were won by Christ's love.

Life took on an entirely different meaning. They were new. Their marriage was new. Back home to put right much that was wrong, they then entered Bible School, followed by missionary orientation and two years of language study in Jordan, before moving out, in May 1979, with their three girls, to witness for Christ in the Middle East.

"Father, when *will* the gods come out and eat this food?"

Young Ramesh Timotheus dutifully laid out food for the idols on the family altar before attempting to take the first meal of the day himself. He tried so hard to "have faith". His father, a devout Hindu and proud of his caste, had told him that if he had real faith the gods would emerge from the idols and eat the food offered to them.

"It never happened," Ramesh told us. "I offered food regularly and prayed fervently but no sign of approval from the gods ever came my way. We had come to India from Pakistan at the time of partition, and my dear mother died when I was nine. Father had remarried and home became an unhappy place for me. I was lonely and afraid, and even the gods could not meet my need."

Ramesh was eventually sent to live with an uncle who taught him long Sanskrit prayers and ritualistic bathing. He took part in a special Hindu ceremony, being taught a "mantra" for daily incantation – but his nature was untouched and he grew up into evil practices.

At eleven, he was apprenticed to a tailor in Kanpur, working long hours making buttonholes and sewing hems.

The years only brought him increasing frustration and restlessness.

"When I was seventeen," Ramesh recalls, "I saw a newspaper advertisement: 'Precious but free – the life story of Jesus Christ.' I knew nothing about Christianity but, because it was free, I wrote off and received a John's Gospel and a correspondence course. In spite of violent objections from my brother and criticism from my work-mates, I completed this and other courses. I even considered becoming a Christian – but if God wanted me to be a Christian, would I not have been born into a Christian home?

"I started to attend Christian meetings. I heard people who had been born into Christian homes saying that they only became Christians when they were 'born again'. What was it all about? During prayer time one day, I heard God's voice saying: 'Ramesh, *you* need to be born again.' Hardly understanding what it meant, I prayed: 'Lord, I want to be born again. Please forgive me and cleanse me.' I rose from my knees with great joy and peace flooding my whole being."

Ramesh continued in the tailor's shop for some time, witnessing to family and friends (including the Middletons!), but the voice of God was becoming insistent that he should move into full-time Christian service. Where could he get some training? He met some WEC missionaries who told him of the Tasmania Missionary Training College. So he and his devoted wife Lajwanti sent off their application papers, and were accepted in Tasmania. While in Australia, God's voice came again and told them to "Go West!"

Since 1977 they have been part of the team working in the British Midlands amongst the Asian community. Many have already been won to Christ, but not without persecution and threats to the little family and their home. Despite this, Ramesh has been privileged under God to establish a thriving church community of over one hundred members, for which he has trained and prepared indigenous leadership.

1980 – Missionaries in technicolor

"Whatever else we learned at Intercon '78," wrote one field leader, "the major problem is clear. There are still millions of people who have never heard the gospel. With our present missionary workforce, we will never be able to reach them."

At last, WEC had realised that she would have to look in *two* directions to solve this problem. Firstly, there were still untapped reserves of personnel in the evangelical churches of the *West*, who needed a touch from God to stir them out of their apathy and indifference as spectators, into the excitement of becoming participants in the arena. Home base personnel would have to seek new ways of implanting a zeal for missions, a concern for the lost, a willingness for involvement in the gigantic effort of making Christ known to every remaining unreached people group before the end of this century.

Secondly, WEC (and all other missionary societies) would also have to look to the growing churches in the so-called "Third World", where there were ninety-two million committed or mature Christians. It was essential that every one of the new indigenous churches should become a missionary church, training and sending out and supporting missionaries. These Christian communities were strong, full of vibrant zeal for the Word and work of God. Now they had to be motivated to tackle the unfinished task, to fulfil Christ's last great commission to His disciples.

To do this, they would need guidance as to what sort of missionaries would be acceptable in other lands; what constituted the characteristics of a twentieth-century ambassador of Christ; and how to select, train and support such a person from a local assembly of believers.

"At a recent meeting in Japan", Pastor Ruichi Nakazawa spoke thoughtfully, yet with an infectious smile lighting up his face, "the missionaries spoke of the kind of *gifts* that new workers should have, whereas we Japanese spoke of the kind of *person* we need."

He was speaking on the subject of the needed qualifications of a modern-day missionary, at the Kilcreggan Conference, and he carefully and quietly enumerated certain essential characteristics.

"We need missionaries who can show us what we must do, and then lead us to do that work. We ourselves need to be more involved in God's work, not having it all done for us.

"When I look over the history of evangelism in Japan," he said, "I see that, more than the work of leading many people to Christ, the training of a few pastors, evangelists, church elders and laymen has been the most fruitful. The groups who put their efforts into producing leaders were not very outstanding in the beginning, but now they are the ones who are growing and bearing fruit.

"For this type of work, we need people with a deep spirituality and a life of prayer. The ministry is work that brings to birth and gives life. It is spiritual warfare. It is therefore reasonable that the worker be a man who is moved by God through prayer, and not one who runs round in his own strength.

"Then he needs a heart to nurture and train others. It is important to have a parent heart rather than a teacher heart, a heart that loves God's children, that desires their growth and that counts it a joy to make whatever sacrifice is necessary for that growth. The man who has the aptitude not only to manage and control his own gifts, but also to supervise, lead, discipline and train the gifts of the flock, is the man who will be greatly used.

"A leader has to be someone who proves himself worthy of another's trust and confidence. A talented speaker and special gifts will draw an audience but unless a worker can win confidence in special relationships, there will be no disciples. The ministry is not attracting spectators, but making disciples of Christ.

"Then, it is essential that a worker be a good example. Japanese are great copiers. They borrow ideas from the

West and in no time they produce something peculiarly Japanese for export on the world market.

"With regard to the spread of the gospel, this is how Japanese need to be touched. Japanese business men are much more interested in being shown a sample than in receiving an instruction booklet or listening to a lecture. Though it is good to distribute literature and have foreign speakers give good messages, it is much more profitable to have a missionary sent to us as a living example of a servant and a witness of God. I don't mean to say that we are waiting for perfect saints to arrive. If they'll invite us to be honest about them, to please God and not to be discouraged, to make the Cross of Christ their resting place, to be patient in hardship, to believe, to love, to serve – it is this attitude that has a tremendous power of influence.

"Finally, may I remind you that Paul spoke to Timothy about his attitudes, not about his gifts, when he said: 'Set the believers an example in speech and conduct, in love, in faith, in purity.'"

1981 – Training the future workers

How could these new-type missionaries be trained?

C. T. Studd had his own version of a Bible School in the Congo. Jack Harrison developed it and many pastors and evangelists have been trained at Ibambi in the sixty years of WEC ministry there. But changes were needed.

Pastor Nonziodane returned to Zaïre from Intercon '78 with a burning vision for training the educated young people of his country, not only for the pastoral ministry and for teaching in the Bible Schools, but also for missionary work in other lands. Others caught his enthusiasm, and the Church decided to launch the Isiro Bible Institute. Ron and Ev Sims (Australia) were appointed to assist Pastor Nonziodane, who had already been trained at the AIM (Africa Inland Mission) Theological College at Bunia.

In Tasmania, the WEC Missionary Training College was founded in 1956. Shortly afterwards, Stewart and Marie Dinnen joined the staff as Principals, and over 400 students have been trained, 67 per cent going into overseas missionary work. All the staff are full members of WEC, all with a deep burden for mission, which is kept constantly before the students. Potential missionaries need to know the Bible and be given a key to the many sciences important for Christian service. They are kept in touch with world realities and prepared specifically for them.

At the British WEC Headquarters, Dave and Anne Burnett have brought to birth a Missionary Orientation Centre (MOC), where students from all over the world come to be prepared for service in their own countries or as cross-cultural missionaries. Special courses deal with all the major religions: others handle the new sciences of cultural anthropology, missiology and church growth, enabling missionaries to understand and communicate meaningfully to those of another culture, and to plant and build up national churches. Sarah and Samuel Kang from Korea were among the first graduates from MOC, having already attended a seminary in Korea. When they left England for missionary service in Nigeria, they testified to the enormous benefit they had gained from the courses at Bulstrode.

The Christian Service College at Kumasi in central Ghana grew from small beginnings. In 1972, the original vision came to Greg Francis, that a college was needed to train national workers to take their place alongside the missionaries in the local churches. The idea mushroomed. Now they are training men and women from any part of West Africa to go anywhere that the Lord would call them. They sent a call to Bill and Myra Chapman, at that time Principals of the WEC MTC in Glasgow: "Come over and help us!"

For the Chapmans, it meant sacrifice right from the start, but they had been gripped by the vision and invested all they had in its fulfilment. A group of Ghanaian business men accepted responsibility as a Council of Reference, and evening classes started in January 1974. Bill lost the sight of one eye, and had to fly home to Britain for emergency surgery; but undeterred, he was soon back at the job. Isaac and Grace Ababio joined them in the ministry. Just back from theological training in Australia and teaching experience in New Guinea, this mature Ghanaian couple proved a tremendous asset. By 1980, over thirty young men had received their diplomas or certificates, and all were in key places in the Lord's work in Ghana or other West African countries.

In Java, Lynne Newell has become deeply involved in the South East Asia Bible Seminary. Called to Java by the testimony of a young Unevangelized Fields Mission (UFM) missionary on furlough from the college in 1956, Lynne completed her Bible College and missionary orientation training with WEC, and reached Java in 1958. Busy in language study and adapting to the village culture of the Javanese, Lynne was at first unprepared for the call to join the team at the seminary, but the Lord was persistent. In 1960, she went as a stop-gap during the furlough of the very UFM missionary through whom she had heard God's call to serve in Java. On returning to Java after her first furlough, Lynne became a full-time faculty member of the seminary in 1964. For the next ten years, she helped train students for a Diploma of Theology. Steadily the standard of training rose, till the seminary was offering a degree course for a Master of Arts in Religious Studies.

In 1978, the Principal encouraged Lynne, with the full support of the WEC missionaries in Java, to go to Westminster Theological Seminary in Philadelphia for four years of further study. "Although I felt a bit long in the tooth", wrote Lynne, "to be commencing studies in Hebrew etc., I just knew that this was God's plan for me." Equipped now with a Master's degree in Theology, Lynne has once again returned, with great joy, to the Javanese Seminary and to the training of national pastors and missionaries.

So there is no shortage of possibilities for the training of would-be missionaries. All over the world, WEC missionaries are helping in Bible Schools and Christian Service colleges and seminaries, in Missionary Training Colleges and Orientation Centres for the training of national evangelists and cross-cultural missionaries, students coming from many different countries and going to serve in as many different churches and societies.

1982 – Portugal's hour of opportunity

At the beginning of the twentieth century a handful of workers toiled in Portugal amidst hostility and persecution. Then the door was slammed shut, the opportunity was lost, darkness reigned.

In the 1970s, the people of Portugal rose up against the oppression of a system that was crushing them, a war that was bleeding their economy and manpower, a lifestyle that was the most backward of any in Europe. April 25th, 1974 was to be indelibly written into the hearts of the Portuguese as the day when freedom came to Portugal.

With revolutionary freedom came religious freedom. People freed from shackles, disillusioned with politicians, questioning the validity of the State Church and uncertain of the future, were desperately seeking for answers, open to talk, discuss and listen. A huge spiritual vacuum had developed, especially among the young.

Through this open door poured all the sects and cults. Mormons, Moonies and Witnesses; Children of God, Hari Krishna and Divine Light; all going from door to door and mixing on the streets, with their hand-out literature.

Where was the Church of Jesus Christ? In general, the Church was desperately slow to awaken to the opportunities of the hour, that "now is the day of salvation" for Portugal.

George and Trish Baxter felt called to Portuguese-speaking West Africa, and went to Portugal in 1976 for a year of language study. Their early impressions of the country were depressing, but knowing it was only for a limited time, they braced themselves to put up with it.

Then it became clear that God did not want them in West Africa. They checked and re-checked their guidance. All fitted up to their arrival in Portugal, but then what? It was some time before they realised that God was calling them to Portugal itself, not to one of her ex-colonies. But WEC had no base in Portugal. They returned to Britain, only to discover that God had been challenging the leadership to start work in Portugal! The jigsaw was beginning to fit together.

Among the ten million Portuguese, less than 1 per cent were evangelical believers. There was practically no regular gospel witness among the half million northerners. The Baxters moved into the city of Braga in 1979, initially to revitalise the ministry of *Cedo*, the Portuguese broadsheet. During intensive follow-up work from this, they formed small groups of interested friends, who would eventually become the core of new churches. However, the response was very slow.

By 1982, Trish was deeply frustrated by her role – or lack of role – in this situation. "Lord, am I really another Martha that I can't find time to sit at Your feet and enjoy Your presence?" she found herself praying. "I feel so frustrated at times. I wonder what I'm doing here. There doesn't seem to be time to do what's necessary. My girls keep me so occupied, and even they don't get the attention from me that a good mother should give.

"Then there's all the jobs that get left undone – the letters to those who so faithfully pray for us; the new dress I promised to make; that book I've yet to read; even some of yesterday's mail lies unopened on the sideboard!

"Last night I put the alarm on earlier, so I could pray before the day began. Even then, one of the girls was up asking for breakfast. Lord, You know the deep need I feel for spiritual refreshment, and I realise that I can only get it from You."

Modern-day missionary work still demands sacrifice,

faith and holiness, but possibly they need to be re-defined –
the sacrifice of being forgotten, behind-scenes, even lonely,
when you could be secure and successful in your own
homeland: the faith to hold on when there is no sign of fruit,
to believe in God's sovereignty when your immediate world
seems crumbling in ruins around you; the holiness that can
keep bright and shining without anyone watching, when the
hoardings and the television screen reveal only the sordid,
when corruption has seeped into the heart of general
activities and become acceptable to most people.

"The needs around me make me feel so inadequate,
Lord. Remember that lady climbing the steps towards the
church on her knees? I felt I ought to have offered more
than a tract, but my Portuguese is still so far from what I
need to communicate Your gospel. The witch down the
road has no end of people who go to her for help. She has
real influence. I'd like to think my life had influence for
You, Lord.

"Lord, the noise all last night – I couldn't sleep. I'm
beginning to shout at the children. I need You, Lord, to
keep me clean and make me holy."

There was all the idolatry, the lack of literature, the
appalling poverty, the urgent need of more workers.

Then, through all the distress, Trish suddenly realised
there was the *joy* of being in the centre of God's will.

"I'm so glad, Lord, to know the possibilities of what we
are in You, and the joy we have in working together. The
thought of doing anything else, outside Your will, doesn't
appeal at all. Even my own frustrations seem insignificant
as I realise the darkness around, of those who don't know
You."

1983 – No mistake

"During our first furlough," wrote Harry and Joann
Young, "we were joyfully expecting our first baby. But on
May 7th, 1960 when our dear son, Terry, was born, without

legs or proper hands and with tiny arms, our hearts cried out, 'How will he ever cope?'"

"Quietly God came with His own assurance", Joann continued, "that this was no mistake. While still in hospital He comforted me through Isaiah 43:7, 'I have created him for my glory, I have formed him, yea, I have made him.'"

"But what of our call and commitment to the mission field?" they both queried. "Had our first term with its language learning and knowledge gained of the people and customs been in vain?"

"As we waited on the Lord," Harry said, "the strong conviction settled on our hearts that God had not withdrawn His call. He was asking us to follow through faithfully and to take Terry with us. He gave us the promise: 'If you will believe, you will see the glory of God.'"

"The great agony of choice did not hit me until our second furlough," Joann confessed. "Terry was admitted to a special hospital in the USA to be fitted with artificial legs. After many months of fitting and training, he was at last able to walk. By this time he had started school. My heart was torn. 'Am I right as a mother to take my child from an excellent school and hospital, back to Dubai (then little more than a desert sheikhdom) where there is neither school nor hospital suitable for him?'

"Clearly God's Word came: 'Go, I will take care of Terry's schooling and medical treatment.' It was a step of faith. God's amazing provision for us – from the daily visits of the British Agent's governess to teach Terry, to the airlift to Britain at the time of the June 6th war, enabling Terry to be enrolled at Roehampton, one of the finest hospitals in the world for amputees – is a wonderful story."

And Terry? What has he to say?

"It was on my trip home from Arabia with my Dad, to attend school and have my artificial legs renewed (I outgrew legs as well as trousers!) that I became a Christian. I wondered what would happen if the plane crashed and I had to meet God. There and then, up in the air, I asked Jesus to become my Saviour and take over my life.

"That was only the beginning of proving God's help in everyday life. I was becoming more aware of people's reaction to my disability and had to learn early that being stared at was part of my life.

"Whereas I used to regard my artificial legs as a nuisance to be endured only to please the grown-ups, I am now so grateful to my parents for *making* me wear them. They have become my passport into the 'normal' world.

"Someone once asked how I coped, with being handicapped and being a Christian. I find that these are two basically different questions. You see, God has more than fulfilled His promise to meet all my needs. He has given me great parents, brothers and sisters, a good education, and lately, though much less importantly, a brand new car – as well as a host of other benefits.

"But God's more interested in the kind of person He can make me than He is in the number of things He can give me. If I meet a problem in *doing* things, I have to take it as it comes, and God is very good at helping me solve this type of problem. It is the problem of *myself* and what I *am* that is most troublesome, but He is working in this realm too!

"One of my problems has been taking credit that I don't deserve when God answers prayer and blesses in a special way. I did well at school and in exams [Terry gained ten O-levels and five A-levels, and now has a Ph.D. in physics from Birmingham University]; and even though I had prayed a lot about these things beforehand, I used to forget to give the credit back where it belonged. I so easily became complacent about success, even though I know that without God's help, I would be a complete flop."

God taught Terry this lesson very clearly when he failed his driving test. He had been so keen to become independent and took for granted that God would allow him to drive himself to lectures at university. He was shattered when he did not pass the test. "I don't think things had ever looked quite so black before," he confessed. What had gone wrong? Hadn't they all prayed about it?

"One or two things then became clearer," Terry testified. "First of all, God never promised me a life of unqualified success. If I am going to be a Christian just for the good things God gives me, then my experience is going to be very lopsided and my understanding of Him shallow. Secondly, I cannot see beyond the present. The 'what-might-have-beens' remain with God. Where He allows one thing to happen rather than another, I know I can trust the decision because I can trust the Decider." (Terry passed his driving test, next time round!)

"I believe strongly that God has a plan for my life. Just what exactly this will turn out to be, I do not know yet. What I do know is that He is out for the absolute best for me. So far He has strewn my way with blessings and I am sure He does not intend stopping now. 'The Lord will fulfil His purpose for me; Your love, O Lord, endures for ever – do not abandon the works of Your hands'" (Psalm 138:8).

"As I look back", Joann mused when on furlough in the States in 1983, "how easy it would have been in the early days to shelter Terry – no travel, no new situations, no probing questions, no distressing decisions. Yet the constraint of the Spirit of God would not sanction the 'secure' life.

"God in His great wisdom, saw to it that Terry's personality and spirit developed in a framework of a full family life. Friends in the Gulf – Indians, Arabs, British, Americans – who passed in and out, added a dimension to life that would have been missing in a confined situation.

"Has God been faithful to His promises? Has He answered that question: 'Will Terry ever be able to cope?' Indeed, exceedingly abundant has been His answer. Our greatest joy is in Terry's steadfast faith in the Lord and his willing service for Christ, who has turned seeming tragedy into triumph."

1984 – Jobs galore!

"Can an older mission like WEC recapture the momentum it had in the fifties and sixties?" Stewart Dinnen answered emphatically, "Yes! If we can couple our maturity, stability and expertise with the energy and drive of a new generation of workers, we will make a significant contribution to the accomplishment of the greatest task on earth – winning the lost for Christ."

Once again, the leadership of WEC fields and WEC-related churches from all around the world had gathered at Kilcreggan for an intensive three weeks of conference. Events had moved so fast in the past six years that it was patently impossible to wait until 1988 for "Intercon II" as had been originally envisaged. During the conference, called to discuss future strategies and policies, God out-lined exciting new developments and put a holy boldness in all hearts to claim His enabling for a new forward thrust.

Patrick Johnstone, the Deputy International Secretary, gave an astonishing survey of world needs within the reach of present WEC endeavours, and then spelt out to the hundred delegates, region by region, the possibilities for advance. Unreached peoples were identified: unevangel-ised cities were earmarked for entry; new methods of outreach in project teams were proposed; and the chal-lenge of some areas not in the present WEC sphere of service were considered.

Particular attention was drawn to forty-four unevangel-ised peoples, mainly within reach of existing programmes; and to thirty-nine new urban and city areas needing to be entered and won for Christ. It was also noted that, in the final crunch, the bottleneck in missions was not money or machinery, but men and women who know what true discipleship means, ready to go wherever the Lord directs, sensitive to the Spirit's leading and full of faith to act on the promises of God.

Conference split up and met in regional groups for in-depth study sessions. By careful and prayerful analysis, proposals for advance were outlined and commitments to steps of faith were taken.

The Africa regional group, with 280 field workers in 1984, recognised the need to double that figure if the advance programmes contemplated in Ivory Coast, Zaïre, Senegal, the Gambia, Chad, Liberia, Burkino Faso, Ghana, Guinea Bissau and Equatorial Guinea were to be achieved. By God's enabling, twenty-five new people groups were to be entered, and churches planted in eleven new cities. Guinea (Conakry) was specially noted as an area for immediate advance. CAPRO, a sister-mission based in Nigeria, planned to co-operate with WEC and establish a bridgehead in Guinea just as soon as possible.

The South America regional group recognised a need in each of their three fields for reinforcements for church planting and for the training of nationals to become missionaries. The Brazilian team saw exciting possibilities ahead of sending Brazilians to Guinea Bissau and other needy areas.

The Europe regional group determined to plant four new churches in and around Madrid in the following five years. For advance in the northern region of Italy, a steady stream of couples would be needed, willing to become wholly integrated into the local churches. The French team were trusting God to send two or three couples every two years, into their church planting ministry and the planned outreach to students and Muslims. Portugal needed reinforcements for consolidation of the present work. Greece, "the least evangelised country of Europe" (apart from Albania), was to be researched with a view to possible entry.

The East Asia regional group stated that in Japan, the church and missionaries were trusting God for twenty new workers to enter a new, quite unreached area to the south-west of their present work. In Indonesia, the WEC would continue to work in close harmony with the Indonesian Missionary Fellowship, who needed two more qualified teachers at the college as well as some twenty others for church planting ministry. In Singapore, Hong Kong, Taiwan and the Philippines, the mission's main ministry was that of challenging the existing Chinese churches and helping them to train and prepare their missionary candidates.

The South Asia regional group formulated plans for a new thrust in North India, requiring a dozen workers. The visa situation made this a tremendous challenge to faith. WEC had an invitation to join others working in Sri Lanka, and would expect six workers there by 1990. A faith target was set of sixteen new workers for Pakistan. In Thailand, one of the mission's largest fields, the team had faith to see three new churches planted each year for the next five years. Twenty new workers would be needed.

The Middle East regional group could not publish details of their plans, but trusted to double its personnel in its present spheres of activity and to open up several more with workers going out under a Special Overseas Service (SOS) scheme.

Patrick summed up all the findings and faith targets, in an awe-inspiring plenary session. To meet the challenge for extension, as well as maintaining all present commitments, eight hundred new workers would be needed within the next six years. God gave a great witness of the Spirit to the united gathering that this was of *Him*, and not of man, and the whole family rose to their feet to acknowledge their faith in God to do the impossible, and to bring into the visible what was then only visionary.

The acceptance of this challenge, "800 in the 80s", has driven the worldwide family of WEC to their knees with the cry: "Lord, put the thrust-jets of Your Holy Spirit behind hundreds of quality young men and women so that they will join us. Then You will accomplish through us in the many valleys what You have shown us on the mountain top!"

"Jobs galore!" commented Stewart. "What a paradox! In the day of the dole queue, mission is one vast, glorious 'job-centre'!"

1985 – From all the Church to all the World

By 1985, WEC had already accepted into its ranks full-time missionaries from many different racial and cultural backgrounds, and exciting testimonies were coming from all parts of the world as to the special contribution this new dimension was giving to the ministry.

From Zimbabwe to Japan: Newman Mzvondiwa had been conscious of a clear call to Japan for some time, but he had to overcome many obstacles before he could reach his destination. As a member of the Evangelical Church in Zimbabwe, he attended their Bible College and then applied to WEC in South Africa. From their headquarters and missionary training course, he came to Bulstrode, UK, for final acceptance into the mission. While in London, he attended the local Japanese Church for a year. When he reached Japan in 1983, he was given a most warm welcome by the local church, and felt very much at home with them. He oriented well and was found to have a unique contribution to make to Japan. Before returning to Zimbabwe for his first furlough, he had the joy of seeing Japanese putting their trust in Christ as Saviour, as a direct result of his ministry.

From Hong Kong to the Gambia: "I came from a Buddhist family," Daniel Hui testified, "and became a Christian at sixteen, through a Billy Graham Crusade meeting in my home town of Hong Kong in 1975. At once I wanted to tell others!"

The testimonies of Hudson Taylor and Isobel Kuhn challenged this young Christian, as did those of all who suffered for their faith. When he saw the devotion to duty of Buddhist monks, Mormons and Jehovah's Witnesses, he felt ashamed of the lukewarmness of Christians. "I knew God was preparing me for full-time service, yet I found it hard to submit my will to His."

Daniel's call to serve in WEC came when he was at Bible School, through a student who had attended missionary orientation courses at Bulstrode. A talk with Robert

Mackey when he was visiting the WEC workers in Hong Kong in 1982 opened Daniel's eyes to the needs of the Gambia. Reading the biography of C. T. Studd and other WEC literature confirmed to Daniel that he should join the WEC fellowship. Backed by his home church, he came to the UK in September 1982 to do his candidate's training; and eventually flew to the Gambia in June 1984.

"It can be discouraging", Daniel wrote humbly in 1985, "when I evaluate my achievements, and find few tangible results: but I realise that God is more interested in my faithfulness than in visible results. In this Muslim land of the Gambia, fruit has been hard to produce: yet I want to be His faithful servant."

From Brazil to Sri Lanka: Fatima Amorim grew up in a Baptist church, but her teen years were traumatic. Her wealthy father, who had been the local leader of both the Baptist church and also the freemasonry lodge, lost all his money, left the church and forced his family to do the same. Spiritism, Freemasonry and Bible reading were freely mixed to find answers to their many problems, and led to ever increasing confusion. Fatima began to hate everything to do with Christianity, and more than once sought to take her life.

A woman spoke with her; her Christian mother was praying for her; her heart had reached rock-bottom, and she cried out: "God, if You are, reveal Yourself to me!" and quite simply, He did, and she knew that she was born again. Finishing school and working as a secretary, there was a growing desire in her heart for full-time Christian service. Her parents were not in agreement, as she was then the only breadwinner in the family. However, trusting them to God, she went to Bible College, where, amongst many other missions, she heard of WEC, and also of the need for workers in Sri Lanka. It took five years' patient waiting and watching, before the Lord eventually opened the door for her to move forward to this land.

In January 1985, she eventually flew to Sri Lanka, at the invitation of another Christian group, to help in a hospital, though she had no medical training whatsoever! It was "an open door" and she went through it at the Lord's command. Though she found the work hard, the life lonely, the problem of communicating either in her awkward English or in the intensely difficult Sinhalese language almost insurmountable, nevertheless she knew she was where God wanted her.

From Taiwan to Venezuela: Though Samuel Yang was raised in a Christian home, he was eighteen before he realised that Christianity was not just a religion, but had to be applied to his life to be meaningful. Entering a seminary in Taiwan, and reading missionary magazines displayed in the library, he started to pray that God would send out labourers into His harvest field. Slowly it registered that God wanted to answer that prayer by sending him, Samuel, overseas!

Few if any Taiwanese had ever gone abroad as missionaries. Could this be possible? His professors tried to discourage him: there would be the problem of learning English: China was a vast mission field, so no society would accept him for anywhere else. He wrote to various missionary societies, but none responded to the idea of accepting a Taiwanese into their ranks.

One day, on his way to church, he picked up a stray piece of paper, tore it across and stuffed it in his pocket. Arriving early, he pulled the scraps out and read: "Don't throw this away!" Piecing it together, he read a challenge to Chinese Christians to serve God as cross-cultural missionaries. It was the first Chinese edition of *Look!* He contacted the editor, and at last received some encouragement.

During his pastoral internship, he married Nancy, a school-teacher member of his church and one who shared his vision. Seminary-trained in music, she became an excellent helpmeet to Samuel. They entered missionary candidates' training in WEC's London Headquarters in 1985, to prepare for future service in Venezuela in South America.

1986 – Operation World!

"We look back over our sixteen years in Africa," wrote Patrick and Jill Johnstone in 1980, "with gratitude for all the lessons we have learned and also for the joys we have experienced in God's service in the Dorothea Mission. Now the Lord has led us in thrilling ways to the WEC fellowship, including a year's service with Operation Mobilisation on board mv Logos."

Patrick had been invited to the 1978 Kilcreggan WEC conference, at a time when Leslie Brierley was scouring the world for someone to succeed him as International Research Secretary. Patrick and Jill were seeking the Lord for guidance for their future ministry, as Africans were fully ready to take over the leadership of the Church's evangelistic ministry in Zimbabwe. The Dorothea Mission were most gracious in agreeing to this change-over, seeing it as part of the Lord's blueprint for the final thrust of missions before the close of the twentieth century.

"It is a new and harsh world that we face," Patrick commented, as he looked out on the world of the 1980s. "A world of advancing communism, resurgent Islam and Hinduism, closing doors, visa crises for missionaries. We see the decline of Christianity in the West before a permissive, materialistic humanism. The Body of Christ is sinking into lethargy, sinful ignorance and cowardly evasion of the Great Commission. World evangelisation is *not* complete, and there remains yet much land to be possessed. Where are the Calebs who will cry out, 'Let us go up at once and possess it, for we are well able to overcome it'?

"We need to enthuse believers," he continued, with his own bubbling and infectious enthusiasm, "with the exhilarating challenge of going out to disciple the nations. Opportunities still abound and will continue to do so until Jesus comes again. Our task must be seen to be realisable in *this* generation. It is going to cost us to do it, but anything worthwhile is always costly."

There was a growing realisation of a need to broaden the

recruitment for missionary work – to accept tent-making missionaries, students, tourists, short-termers, believers from all continents, pastors and others. There was a need for flexibility and mobility in the light of the rapid and traumatic changes going on all over the world. "Are we keeping one pace *ahead* of events, or lagging woefully behind, caught half-asleep and unprepared?"

"We need to have a new humility and adaptability," said Patrick, "in the light of ever more insistent demands for a presentation of the gospel that has no foreign accretions, as we seek to assault the major unevangelised blocs of the world – the lands of Buddhists, Muslims and Hindus."

One of Patrick's tasks on joining WEC was to rewrite the magnificent guide to praying for the world, *Operation World*, that he had first compiled while with the Dorothea Mission in Zimbabwe.

In 1900, Andrew Murray had written *The Key to the Missionary Problem*, in which he challenged Christians and churches to hold a "Week of Prayer for the World". It would seem that this challenge was never implemented. In 1943, Hans von Staden, preaching the gospel in the rapidly developing urban slums of Southern Africa, brought to birth the Dorothea Mission. Prayer was a major tool in this mission under von Staden's leadership.

In 1962, they arranged the first of what was to become over one hundred "Weeks of Prayer for the World", in Africa and Europe. Patrick took part in the very first such week. A year later, organising a similar week in Nairobi, he became deeply aware of the need for prayer information if the week was to have real value. The sheets of facts and figures then put together became the forerunner of today's *Operation World*.

When, in 1970, Hans von Staden proposed a new edition, little did Patrick know what he was getting involved in! The work which began in odd moments in the midst of a busy itinerant ministry, using two cardboard boxes in the back of a van as filing cabinets, grew at an alarming pace. In 1976, Operation Mobilisation prepared prayer cards to accompany the book and so help busy people pray intelligently. Translations of *Operation World* into several other languages began to take place.

Having joined WEC in 1980, the mammoth task of gathering relevant information went on. He now had the use of libraries and information from sources all over the world, and could employ the most modern technology for the storing and sorting of all such information. It took him and his willing team of helpers "three years, thousands of letters, hundreds of thousands of pages of reading, and months of typing, checking and editing of the manuscript" to have the fourth edition ready to be sent out in 1986. Their fervent prayer is that it will mobilise Christians around the world to pray for the completion of the Great Commission before the turn of the century.

1987 – "Let us go up at once and possess it!"

Should we not enter Fiji? The question, proposed at the 1984 Kilcreggan Conference, had lain in abeyance for a year.

Bhim Singh, a South African Indian, was trained at the WEC Tasmanian MTC, where he received his marching orders from God for Mauritius. During his first term in this island world, Bhim married a lovely Chinese girl, which necessitated their return to South Africa. Seeking the Lord for the next step in their lives, God directed them towards the dominion of Fiji. Over half the population there are Indians, the descendants of imported indentured labour at the turn of the century. This largely Hindu community, dominating all commercial activities, especially that of the sugar industry, is almost unreached by the gospel.

The South Pacific Evangelical Mission (SPEM) had been working in Fiji for many years, but through force of circumstances the Home Board had to wind up its activities. In 1985, Ken Getty, Canadian WEC leader, received a

letter from the Board, asking if SPEM could be amalga-
mated with WEC. As a result, Mr and Mrs Cairns, SPEM's
one remaining couple, joined WEC and became the first
WEC field leaders in Fiji!

Carol Whipp was accepted by WEC Australia in 1983, to
go to India with a new venture arranged in fellowship
between WEC and Operation Mobilisation. After tackling
Hindi and feeling happily settled into the Indian culture,
Carol's visa was withdrawn and she had to leave. Returning
to the UK, she wondered what God had for her. Was all the
hard slog of language study to be of no avail?

"Will you prayerfully consider working among the
Hindi-speaking Indian community in Fiji?" WEC
leadership asked Carol.

The jigsaw was beginning to fit together! South African
Bhim Singh and his Chinese wife, with experience among
Indians in Mauritius: Australian Carol Whipp, with Hindi
language study in India: a Canadian couple and a New
Zealand couple are all moving to join the Cairns in Fiji, to
take up the challenge of presenting the gospel to the
quarter of a million Indians resident there.

Should we not enter Guinea? Again the question was
proposed at the 1984 Kilcreggan Conference, and this time,
there was an immediate response.

Guinea is surrounded by countries where WEC works –
Senegal, Guinea Bissau, Liberia and Ivory Coast. A wide-
open door for missions was proclaimed by the new government in April 1984 following the overthrow of the previous
Marxist regime. Discussions were already under way
between protestant missions on co-operation for the
evangelisation of the land.

As a result of discussions at Kilcreggan, Bayo Famonure,
leader of CAPRO, a Nigerian Mission, visited the Guinea-
Bissau church conference in October 1984 to discuss a
co-operative venture into the coastal area of Guinea.

Mike and Margaret Dawson felt the call of God to move

in, and start this new field of operations. Soon afterwards, David Cuthbert knew that that was where God wanted him to serve. Things were moving.

"As we lumbered in second gear up the rocky riverbed," wrote Helen Kennedy, as she and Alastair visited Guinea in 1986, "we praised the Lord for the Land Rover He had wonderfully supplied to Mike and Margaret." The Kennedys are the WEC Regional Secretaries for Africa, and are closely involved with the advance into Guinea. Having flown to Conakry, the capital, they were now making their way to the Dawsons' home.

Although chaotic conditions seem to reign in the city, "you rarely hear a complaint from the Guineans," wrote Helen, "only thankfulness for liberty and relief that the years of 'slavery' have ended. Mike has a tremendous gift of friendship," Helen's report continued, "and he uses his slowly improving Susu language non-stop."

After language study, what? Where are WEC going in Guinea? "The shouting need is for a Youth Centre in the capital, Conakry," the Kennedys said. "Liberty needs to be channelled constructively, otherwise it becomes licence. Bars and discos, promiscuity and prostitution abound. Pray for a suitable site at a reasonable price: a young couple equipped for youth work: and more co-workers from our sister mission CAPRO. Our burden is for the Susu people, almost a million of them in Lower Guinea, and largely untouched by the gospel."

Should we not enter elsewhere? "I'm sitting by my open window," read a recent magazine article. "It's quite cold now with a fresh light snow falling on the surrounding hills. Traffic is noisy: jeeps and small lorries roll by taking folk to their work. People everywhere, and *dogs*! Quiet now as they sleep in the daytime, but very active at night.

"My accommodation is nice, nine foot by six, just room for a bed and table. I do have a problem sleeping, as my neighbour has a rather active night life, and the walls are very thin board with lots of gaps. Not only does he sing at the top of his drunken voice but brings home company with whom he talks until 2.30 a.m."

"Shopping is easier," explained our unknown friend, "since my helper has taught me to say, 'Oh, that's expensive!' Though I can't yet talk to people, they seem very friendly."

This short extract was written by a missionary who must remain unnamed, from a country which also must remain unnamed: yet can we, in our imagination, grasp the potential of such a situation? There are hundreds of similar opportunities for those who will dare "go up at once and possess" them – daring to lose all that this world holds dear to gain all that God has to offer; daring to accept anonymity here for God's "well done, good and faithful servant" there?

Epilogue

MEN WHO COUNT NOT THEIR LIVES DEAR

WEC has clearly stated their need of "800 new workers during the 80s", to bring their work force to just over 1,700, in order to enter eleven new countries, thirty-nine new cities and forty-four new ethnic groups, as well as maintaining all the present outreach. But what kind of people do these 800 have to be? What qualifications do they need?

It is true that many professional people could fill vital vacancies right now, but professional qualifications are not the priority.

If one looks at the places where the need is, this may help to answer the question about qualifications. The remaining unevangelised areas in the world are among the hardest to win for the Lord Jesus and will demand from all a greater degree of commitment than ever before. The Susu of Guinea, the Baguirmi of Chad, the Baluch of Pakistan, to name but a few, are people who are resistant to the gospel, yet they have had so little chance to hear it.

How are they to be won? By the best soldiers of the Lord Jesus Christ! These soldiers may have to live in places where physical problems and material shortages make basic survival a hard struggle. There will be mental pressures of coping with cultural change, political insecurity and a resistant religion.

Without doubt, the biggest battle will be in the spiritual realm. The clear picture painted so long ago by C. T. Studd, of a warrior doing battle against the evil one and his demons, is still relevant today. "Let us at least make sure, at our death, that the devil holds a thanksgiving service in hell when he hears news of our departure from the field of battle!" Give us men who count not their lives dear unto themselves!

May God send those who are captivated by the love of Christ, lost in wonder at what He has done for them. They need to be disciplined, so that, when the battle gets tough, they won't run away: receptive, appropriating the Lord's resources for their daily walk: prayerful, knowing how to labour in prayer until there is spiritual birth: patient, not looking for instant results: able to take pressure and work well with others, irrespective of background, colour or race. These modern soldiers need to be able to laugh at themselves, and must be willing to give the Lord all the glory for anything achieved.

"Are you tempted to think that only super-spiritual people will do?" wrote Colin Nicholas, Director of British WEC, "and you know you just don't fit into that category? The standard may seem impossible for anyone to achieve. In our own strength, it undoubtedly is, but not for God's Holy Spirit living in us. When *He* has promised to work, we can't make our own inadequacy our excuse.

"We believe", Colin concluded, "that what God wants most are open, willing, teachable and obedient people. He will make them chosen instruments to do His work, right to the uttermost parts of the earth."

"O Breath of Life, come sweeping through us"

O Breath of Life, come sweeping through us,
Revive Thy Church with life and power;
O Breath of Life, come, cleanse, renew us
And fit Thy Church to meet this hour.

O Wind of God, come bend us, break us,
Till humbly we confess our need;
Then in Thy tenderness remake us,
Revive, restore, for this we plead.

O Breath of Love, come breathe within us,
Renewing thought and will and heart;
Come, love of Christ, afresh to win us,
Revive Thy Church in every part.

O Heart of Christ, once broken for us,
'Tis there we find our strength and rest;
Our broken, contrite hearts now solace,
And let Thy waiting Church be blessed.

Revive us, Lord! Is zeal abating
While harvest fields are vast and white?
Revive us, Lord, the world is waiting,
Equip Thy Church to send the Light.

Elizabeth A. P. Head

Conclusion

AND CAN IT BE?

Should anyone have the opportunity to visit the British Headquarters of the WEC International fellowship, at Bulstrode, near Gerrards Cross, they might well be amazed! Turning off the busy A40 road, up a quarter of a mile driveway through farmed parkland, where the sheep have right of way, as one tops the slight incline, suddenly the impressive Tudor mansion comes into view, standing in over thirty acres of well-kept gardens. Entering through the massive front door, the impression of vastness and grandeur increases. Highly polished woodblock flooring, carpeted reception area with comfortable chairs, busy reception desk with a numerous-line telephone switchboard, great carved stairway circling up to the first floor landings, under a mighty dome of glass . . . can this be a mission headquarters?

Central heating throughout, hot and cold water in most of the hundred bedrooms, a well-equipped kitchen, long corridors of offices, many with the most modern technology to increase efficient service . . . is there, perhaps, a mistake?

Maybe it is the well-designed, purpose-built headquarters in Auckland, New Zealand, in its pleasantly landscaped gardens that one has visited: or the ancient Fort, perched commandingly on the Hill overlooking Philadelphia, where the American branch of WEC International have their headquarters, with extensive new buildings all blending into a harmonious and effective whole around the ancient circular water tower.

But where is the sacrifice, you are tempted to ask, to live in such modern, efficient working conditions? How does this side of the picture accord with that of the missionaries on the front line, slogging out an eighteen-hour day in tropical heat and humidity, in a mud hut with beaten earth floor and hard bamboo-bed? Or those slaving away in a crowded tenement building amidst endless noise and interruptions, smells and sights, in down-town Hong Kong, or Bangkok, or Calcutta, or Bogota? Or those waiting for an opportunity to serve, in lonely outposts in so-called closed lands, where they are constantly surrounded by danger and intrigue, hatred and suspicion?

Yet here too, in the busy hubs of the home-end bases of this vast worldwide fellowship of WEC, the same principles, as have guided the mission's service all over the world, are the basis of daily life. In some ways, the sacrifice, faith and holiness demanded of each home-ender, if there is to be a true and powerful fellowship that can be active and creative as God intended it should be, is tougher even than that demanded of those in the far-flung corners of the work.

To live in one small room, with all one's worldly possessions, year after year, as part of a vast and bustling community is far from easy. The demands of the overhead loudspeaker, from early morning to late evening, can be a source of irritation, that must be controlled and subjected to the discipline of acceptance. The need of rotas for domestic duties and as duty driver to and from the airport or hospital with missionaries and staff, can all become wearisome if not submitted to the discipline of obedience. The demands of others on one's time for help or encouragement, for replacement duty or emergency call, can be thought of as a nuisance as one seeks to complete one's own allotted task, unless substituted by the overflowing love of the indwelling Holy Spirit.

Not only does community life demand endless personal *sacrifice*, if local fellowship is to be maintained, but also it is here in the "hubs" that *faith* has to be practised if the worldwide fellowship is to be supported. From all over the world, demands pour in, by letter or by telex, maybe asking for an essential part to repair an urgently needed vehicle in the hinterland of central Africa: maybe informing the community of a need for urgent prayer, such as when a colleague has been imprisoned on a trumped-up charge in a dangerously anti-West country where the death sentence could be summarily imposed. The home-end group must live in such constant, unshakable relationship to the Commander of the mission, that they can go to Him at a moment's notice and ask for that which is needed.

There must be a sincere belief in importunate prayer: a faith to take hold of the answer and thank the Giver, even before it comes into the visible. There has to be a stick-ability and perseverance, a willingness to do battle with the powers of darkness that are arrayed to delay the reception of the answer, until that answer becomes an actuality. There must be profound faith in the availability of the "whole armour of God" for daily warfare, to maintain the health – spiritual and mental, as well as physical – of all the members of the army out at the battle-front and at home in the sending bases.

Holiness in the daily life of each member of these community hubs is another essential ingredient if true fellowship is to be maintained at a deep level, and not merely as a superficial veneer. Without personal holiness, it will be impossible for people to get on with and accommodate to each other, in the intense closeness of these fast-moving, hard-working communities. It is the un-holy bits of character that cause the frictions and "personality incompatibilities".

It is here, at these hubs, that the next generation of missionaries are trained and prepared for battle. If the trainers cannot maintain a God-pleasing standard of personal holiness, how can they expect the trainees to do so? Such things are "caught, not taught". The joyful spirit of service in fulfilling wash-up duty is as important in this respect as effectual, powerful praying in the morning meeting.

And so these centres of *fellowship* seek to supply the front-line with the needed warriors: to channel out the funds and equipment to keep them all fighting fit: to stand behind them in times of fierce conflict as much as during revival blessing: to pray them through the dark periods as much as to praise God with them in the light. It is here that research is endlessly carried on to discover any groups of people still waiting to hear the good news of salvation for the very first time, and the means by which they could be reached. It is here that literature is prepared to educate churches all over the world of these needs, and it is from here that workers go to these same churches to tell and explain such needs, and to stir up prayer and financial support for those who have gone, and a sense of responsibility to send out more of their very best young people to fill some of the enormous gaps still in the ranks.

This is the *raison d'être* of home bases in all missions, who are dedicated to the speediest possible evangelisation of the whole world in the shortest possible time before the return of our King to reign.

Bibliography

Throughout the book, the main source of information has been the bi-monthly magazines of WEC International, British, American, Canadian and Australian; plus personal letters from many of the missionary family of WEC of today. I have also drawn on material in the following books:

Booth, Phil. *Slim Fingers* (Christian Literature Crusade, 1976)

Brierley, Leslie. *First the Blade – World of WEC* (WEC, 1963)

Dinnen, Stewart and Eley, Joan. *God's Brumby* (private, Australia, 1982)

Easton, William. *Colombian Conflict* (Christian Literature Crusade, 1954)

Fenton Hall, Hero and Pioneer – his journals (Christian Literature Crusade, 1925)

Grubb, N. P. *After C. T. Studd* (Lutterworth, 1939)

Grubb, N. P. *Alfred Buxton of Abyssinia and Congo* (Lutterworth, 1942)

Grubb, N. P. *C. T. Studd: Cricketer and Pioneer* (Lutterworth, paperback 1970, hardback 1932)

Grubb, N. P. *Christ in Congo Forests* (Lutterworth, 1945)

Grubb, N. P. *Mighty through God* (Lutterworth, 1951)

Grubb, N. P. *Penetrating Faith in Spanish Guinea* (Evangelical Publishing House, 1941)

Grubb, N. P. *Successor to C. T. Studd* (Lutterworth, 1949)

Macindoe, Betty. *The Desert Blossoms* (Christian Literature Crusade, 1956)

Macindoe, Betty. *Going for God* (Hodder & Stoughton, 1972)

Moules, Len. *Some Want it Tough* (Christian Literature Crusade, 1961)

Moules, Len. *Three Miles High* (Christian Literature Crusade, 1948)

Purves, Jock. *The Unlisted Legion* (Banner of Truth, 1977)

Rowbotham, Elsie. *Would You Believe it?* (WEC, 1963)

Ruscoe, A. W. *The Lame Take the Prey* (Bethany Fellowship, 1968)

Rusha, Gladys. *Truth to Tell – Borneo* (Oliphants, 1969)

Smith, Mrs Gordon. *Victory in Viet Nam* (Zondervan Publishing House, 1965)

Staniford, Frances. *Operation Ivory Coast* (Christian Literature Crusade, 1956)

Studd, C. T. *Reminiscences of Mrs C. T. Studd* (WEC, 1930)

Watt, Eva Stuart. *Floods on Dry Ground* (Marshall, Morgan & Scott, 1939)

Wraight, Pat. *On to the Summit* (Kingsway, 1981)